For the Slow Cooker

Recipes to make your own gifts

Use these recipes to delight your friends and family. Each recipe includes gift tags for your convenience – just cut them out and personalize!

To decorate jars, cut fabric in 9" diameter circles. Screw down the jar

ring to hold fabric in place or hold fabric with a ribbon, raffia, twine, yarn, lace, or string (first secure the fabric with a rubber band before tying). Punch a hole into the corner of the tag and use the ribbon, raffia, twine, yarn, lace, or string to attach the tag to the jar.

These gifts should keep for up to six months. If the mix contains nuts, it should be used within three months.

Printed in the United States of America
by G&R Publishing Co.

Distributed By:

507 Industrial Street
Waverly, IA 50677

ISBN 1-56383-163-5
Item #3009

Rice Pudding Mix

1 1/4 C. white rice
3/4 C. raisins
3/4 C. currants
3/4 C. brown sugar
3/4 C. sugar
1 1/2 tsp. cinnamon

Layer the ingredients in the order given into a wide-mouth 1-quart canning jar. Pack each layer in place before adding the next ingredient.

Attach a gift tag with the cooking instructions.

❀ Use a thin paper plate as a funnel for an easy and no mess way to add ingredients to the jar. ❀

Rice Pudding

1 jar Rice Pudding Mix
1 gallon whole milk

Empty contents of jar into slow cooker, stirring to combine. Heat milk just to boiling point then pour over dry ingredients. Stir well. Cook on high for 3 hours, stirring occasionally especially during the first hour to ensure rice doesn't clump together.

Rice Pudding

1 jar Rice Pudding Mix   **1 gallon whole milk**

Empty contents of jar into slow cooker, stirring to combine. Heat milk just to boiling point then pour over dry ingredients. Stir well. Cook on high for 3 hours, stirring occasionally especially during the first hour to ensure rice doesn't clump together.

Rice Pudding

1 jar Rice Pudding Mix   **1 gallon whole milk**

Empty contents of jar into slow cooker, stirring to combine. Heat milk just to boiling point then pour over dry ingredients. Stir well. Cook on high for 3 hours, stirring occasionally especially during the first hour to ensure rice doesn't clump together.

Rice Pudding

1 jar Rice Pudding Mix   **1 gallon whole milk**

Empty contents of jar into slow cooker, stirring to combine. Heat milk just to boiling point then pour over dry ingredients. Stir well. Cook on high for 3 hours, stirring occasionally especially during the first hour to ensure rice doesn't clump together.

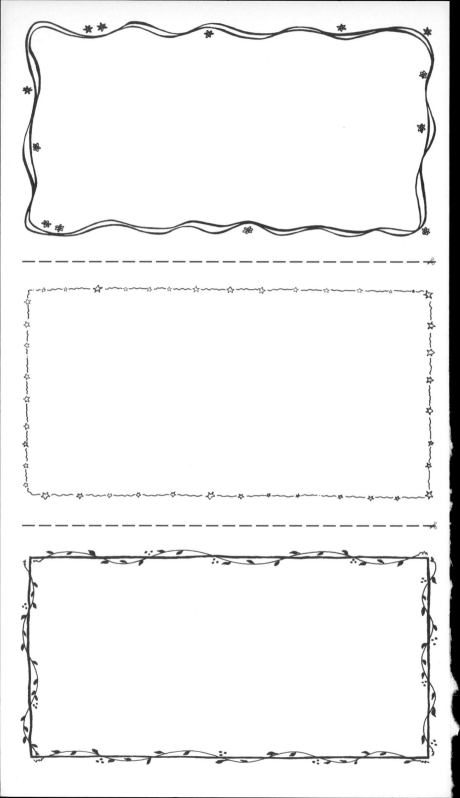

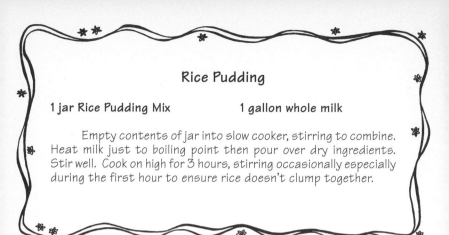

Rice Pudding

1 jar Rice Pudding Mix   **1 gallon whole milk**

Empty contents of jar into slow cooker, stirring to combine. Heat milk just to boiling point then pour over dry ingredients. Stir well. Cook on high for 3 hours, stirring occasionally especially during the first hour to ensure rice doesn't clump together.

Rice Pudding

1 jar Rice Pudding Mix   **1 gallon whole milk**

Empty contents of jar into slow cooker, stirring to combine. Heat milk just to boiling point then pour over dry ingredients. Stir well. Cook on high for 3 hours, stirring occasionally especially during the first hour to ensure rice doesn't clump together.

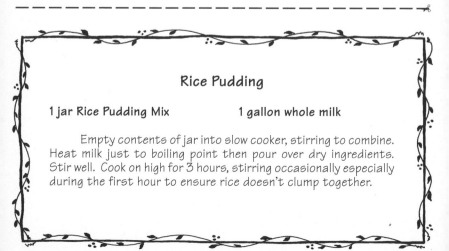

Rice Pudding

1 jar Rice Pudding Mix   **1 gallon whole milk**

Empty contents of jar into slow cooker, stirring to combine. Heat milk just to boiling point then pour over dry ingredients. Stir well. Cook on high for 3 hours, stirring occasionally especially during the first hour to ensure rice doesn't clump together.

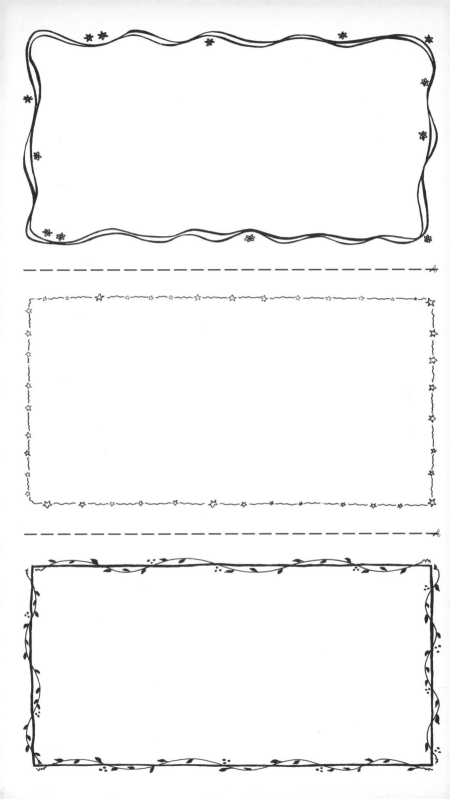

Old Fashioned Ham Hock Stew Mix

1 C. red kidney beans
1 1/3 C. great northern beans
1 C. pinto beans
1 bay leaf (place down the side
of the jar)

Seasoning Packet:

2 T. dried minced onion
2 T. dried celery flakes
1 T. dried parsley
1 tsp. marjoram
1 tsp. dried whole leaf thyme
4 T. chicken bouillon

Layer the ingredients in the order given into a wide-mouth 1-quart canning jar. Mix and place the seasonings in a small plastic bag. Place the packet on top of the beans.

Attach a gift tag with the cooking instructions.

Old Fashioned Ham Hock Stew

1 jar Old Fashioned Ham Hock
   Stew Mix
2 ham hocks (approx. 4 lbs.)
1 C. chopped carrots

Remove seasoning packet from Old Fashioned Ham Hock Stew Mix. Wash beans then place in a microwave safe dish, filling with water 1 to 1 1/2 inches over the beans. Cover tightly with plastic wrap, poking three small holes in the top with a sharp knife. Microwave on high for 9 minutes, rotate and microwave for another 9 minutes. Drain beans, and place in slow cooker. Cover with 10 to 12 cups hot water. Add ham hocks, carrots and seasoning packet. Cook on high for 5 to 6 hours. Remove and discard bay leaf.

Old Fashioned Ham Hock Stew

1 jar Old Fashioned Ham Hock Stew Mix

2 ham hocks (approx. 4 lbs.)
1 C. chopped carrots

Remove seasoning packet from Old Fashioned Ham Hock Stew Mix. Wash beans then place in a microwave safe dish, filling with water 1 to 1 1/2 inches over the beans. Cover tightly with plastic wrap, poking three small holes in the top with a sharp knife. Microwave on high for 9 minutes, rotate and microwave for another 9 minutes. Drain beans, and place in slow cooker. Cover with 10 to 12 cups hot water. Add ham hocks, carrots and seasoning packet. Cook on high for 5 to 6 hours. Remove and discard bay leaf.

Old Fashioned Ham Hock Stew

1 jar Old Fashioned Ham Hock Stew Mix

2 ham hocks (approx. 4 lbs.)
1 C. chopped carrots

Remove seasoning packet from Old Fashioned Ham Hock Stew Mix. Wash beans then place in a microwave safe dish, filling with water 1 to 1 1/2 inches over the beans. Cover tightly with plastic wrap, poking three small holes in the top with a sharp knife. Microwave on high for 9 minutes, rotate and microwave for another 9 minutes. Drain beans, and place in slow cooker. Cover with 10 to 12 cups hot water. Add ham hocks, carrots and seasoning packet. Cook on high for 5 to 6 hours. Remove and discard bay leaf.

Old Fashioned Ham Hock Stew

1 jar Old Fashioned Ham Hock Stew Mix

2 ham hocks (approx. 4 lbs.)
1 C. chopped carrots

Remove seasoning packet from Old Fashioned Ham Hock Stew Mix. Wash beans then place in a microwave safe dish, filling with water 1 to 1 1/2 inches over the beans. Cover tightly with plastic wrap, poking three small holes in the top with a sharp knife. Microwave on high for 9 minutes, rotate and microwave for another 9 minutes. Drain beans, and place in slow cooker. Cover with 10 to 12 cups hot water. Add ham hocks, carrots and seasoning packet. Cook on high for 5 to 6 hours. Remove and discard bay leaf.

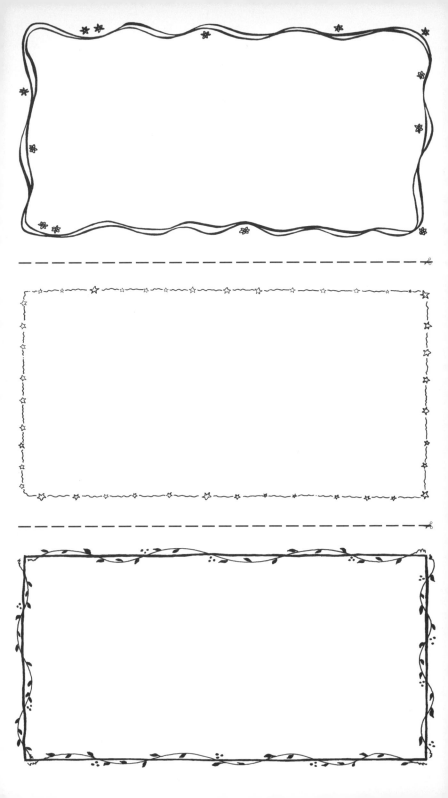

Old Fashioned Ham Hock Stew

1 jar Old Fashioned Ham
  Hock Stew Mix

2 ham hocks (approx. 4 lbs.)
1 C. chopped carrots

Remove seasoning packet from Old Fashioned Ham Hock Stew Mix. Wash beans then place in a microwave safe dish, filling with water 1 to 1 1/2 inches over the beans. Cover tightly with plastic wrap, poking three small holes in the top with a sharp knife. Microwave on high for 9 minutes, rotate and microwave for another 9 minutes. Drain beans, and place in slow cooker. Cover with 10 to 12 cups hot water. Add ham hocks, carrots and seasoning packet. Cook on high for 5 to 6 hours. Remove and discard bay leaf.

Old Fashioned Ham Hock Stew

1 jar Old Fashioned Ham
  Hock Stew Mix

2 ham hocks (approx. 4 lbs.)
1 C. chopped carrots

Remove seasoning packet from Old Fashioned Ham Hock Stew Mix. Wash beans then place in a microwave safe dish, filling with water 1 to 1 1/2 inches over the beans. Cover tightly with plastic wrap, poking three small holes in the top with a sharp knife. Microwave on high for 9 minutes, rotate and microwave for another 9 minutes. Drain beans, and place in slow cooker. Cover with 10 to 12 cups hot water. Add ham hocks, carrots and seasoning packet. Cook on high for 5 to 6 hours. Remove and discard bay leaf.

Old Fashioned Ham Hock Stew

1 jar Old Fashioned Ham
  Hock Stew Mix

2 ham hocks (approx. 4 lbs.)
1 C. chopped carrots

Remove seasoning packet from Old Fashioned Ham Hock Stew Mix. Wash beans then place in a microwave safe dish, filling with water 1 to 1 1/2 inches over the beans. Cover tightly with plastic wrap, poking three small holes in the top with a sharp knife. Microwave on high for 9 minutes, rotate and microwave for another 9 minutes. Drain beans, and place in slow cooker. Cover with 10 to 12 cups hot water. Add ham hocks, carrots and seasoning packet. Cook on high for 5 to 6 hours. Remove and discard bay leaf.

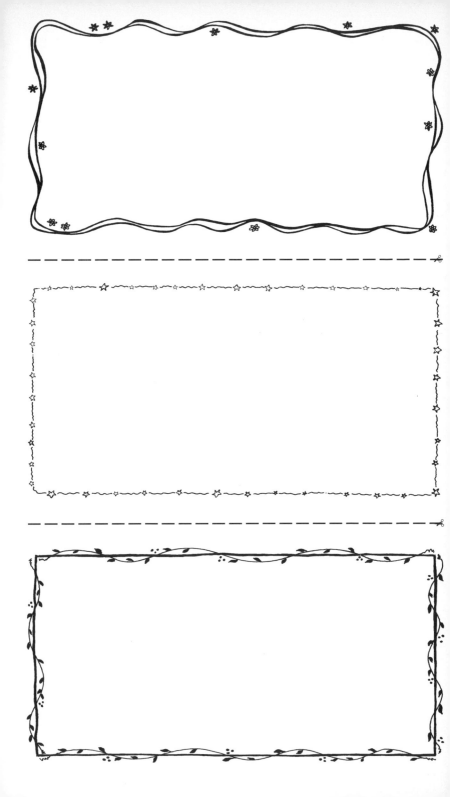

Spanish Red Beans & Rice with Sausage Mix

1 T. dried minced onions
1 tsp. dried minced garlic
1 tsp. cumin
2 tsp. paprika
2 T. chicken bouillon
2 C. white rice

2 C. red beans in a baggie

Layer the ingredients in the order given into a wide-mouth 1-quart canning jar. Place beans on top of the rice.

Attach a gift tag with the cooking instructions.

Spanish Red Beans & Rice with Sausage

1 jar Spanish Red Beans &
   Rice with Sausage Mix
Italian or smoked sausage,
   sliced
1 medium bell pepper, diced

Remove beans from Spanish Red Beans & Rice with Sausage Mix. Wash beans then place in a microwave safe dish, filling with water 1 to 1 1/2 inches over the beans. Cover tightly with plastic wrap, poking three small holes in the top with a sharp knife. Microwave on high for 9 minutes, rotate and microwave for another 9 minutes. Drain beans, and place in slow cooker. Cover with 6 to 8 cups hot water. Cook on high for 3 hours. Brown sausage along with bell pepper. Add sausage mixture along with the remaining Spanish Red Beans & Rice with Sausage Mix. Stir to incorporate. Continue cooking on high for another 1 1/2 hours, stirring occasionally.

Spanish Red Beans & Rice with Sausage

1 jar Spanish Red Beans &
   Rice with Sausage Mix

Italian or smoked sausage, sliced
1 medium bell pepper, diced

Remove beans from Spanish Red Beans & Rice with Sausage Mix. Wash beans then place in a microwave safe dish, filling with water 1 to 1 1/2 inches over the beans. Cover tightly with plastic wrap, poking three small holes in the top with a sharp knife. Microwave on high for 9 minutes, rotate and microwave for another 9 minutes. Drain beans, and place in slow cooker. Cover with 6 to 8 cups hot water. Cook on high for 3 hours. Brown sausage along with bell pepper. Add sausage mixture along with the remaining Spanish Red Beans & Rice with Sausage Mix. Stir to incorporate. Continue cooking on high for another 1 1/2 hours, stirring occasionally.

Spanish Red Beans & Rice with Sausage

1 jar Spanish Red Beans &
   Rice with Sausage Mix

Italian or smoked sausage, sliced
1 medium bell pepper, diced

Remove beans from Spanish Red Beans & Rice with Sausage Mix. Wash beans then place in a microwave safe dish, filling with water 1 to 1 1/2 inches over the beans. Cover tightly with plastic wrap, poking three small holes in the top with a sharp knife. Microwave on high for 9 minutes, rotate and microwave for another 9 minutes. Drain beans, and place in slow cooker. Cover with 6 to 8 cups hot water. Cook on high for 3 hours. Brown sausage along with bell pepper. Add sausage mixture along with the remaining Spanish Red Beans & Rice with Sausage Mix. Stir to incorporate. Continue cooking on high for another 1 1/2 hours, stirring occasionally.

Spanish Red Beans & Rice with Sausage

1 jar Spanish Red Beans &
   Rice with Sausage Mix

Italian or smoked sausage, sliced
1 medium bell pepper, diced

Remove beans from Spanish Red Beans & Rice with Sausage Mix. Wash beans then place in a microwave safe dish, filling with water 1 to 1 1/2 inches over the beans. Cover tightly with plastic wrap, poking three small holes in the top with a sharp knife. Microwave on high for 9 minutes, rotate and microwave for another 9 minutes. Drain beans, and place in slow cooker. Cover with 6 to 8 cups hot water. Cook on high for 3 hours. Brown sausage along with bell pepper. Add sausage mixture along with the remaining Spanish Red Beans & Rice with Sausage Mix. Stir to incorporate. Continue cooking on high for another 1 1/2 hours, stirring occasionally.

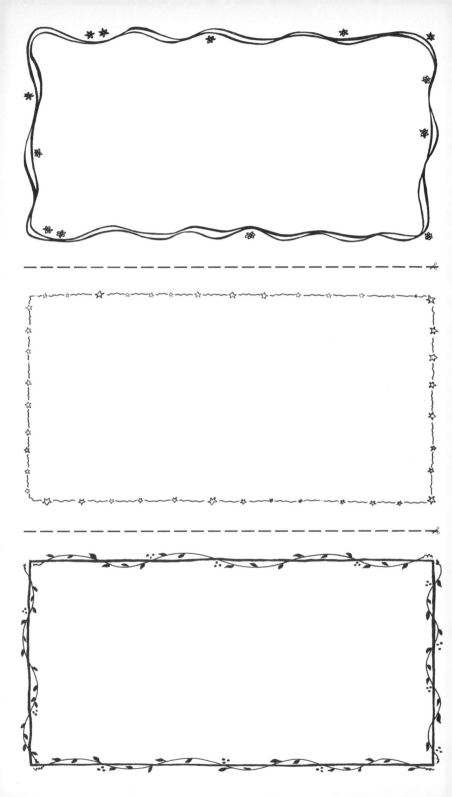

Spanish Red Beans & Rice with Sausage

1 jar Spanish Red Beans & Rice with Sausage Mix

Italian or smoked sausage, sliced
1 medium bell pepper, diced

Remove beans from Spanish Red Beans & Rice with Sausage Mix. Wash beans then place in a microwave safe dish, filling with water 1 to 1 1/2 inches over the beans. Cover tightly with plastic wrap, poking three small holes in the top with a sharp knife. Microwave on high for 9 minutes, rotate and microwave for another 9 minutes. Drain beans, and place in slow cooker. Cover with 6 to 8 cups hot water. Cook on high for 3 hours. Brown sausage along with bell pepper. Add sausage mixture along with the remaining Spanish Red Beans & Rice with Sausage Mix. Stir to incorporate. Continue cooking on high for another 1 1/2 hours, stirring occasionally.

Spanish Red Beans & Rice with Sausage

1 jar Spanish Red Beans & Rice with Sausage Mix

Italian or smoked sausa, sliced
1 medium bell pepper, diced

Remove beans from Spanish Red Beans & Rice with Sausage Mix. Wash beans then place in a microwave safe dish, filling with water 1 to 1 1/2 inches over the beans. Cover tightly with plastic wrap, poking three small holes in the top with a sharp knife. Microwave on high for 9 minutes, rotate and microwave for another 9 minutes. Drain beans, and place in slow cooker. Cover with 6 to 8 cups hot water. Cook on high for 3 hours. Brown sausage along with bell pepper. Add sausage mixture along with the remaining Spanish Red Beans & Rice with Sausage Mix. Stir to incorporate. Continue cooking on high for another 1 1/2 hours, stirring occasionally.

Spanish Red Beans & Rice with Sausage

1 jar Spanish Red Beans & Rice with Sausage Mix

Italian or smoked sausage, sliced
1 medium bell pepper, diced

Remove beans from Spanish Red Beans & Rice with Sausage Mix. Wash beans then place in a microwave safe dish, filling with water 1 to 1 1/2 inches over the beans. Cover tightly with plastic wrap, poking three small holes in the top with a sharp knife. Microwave on high for 9 minutes, rotate and microwave for another 9 minutes. Drain beans, and place in slow cooker. Cover with 6 to 8 cups hot water. Cook on high for 3 hours. Brown sausage along with bell pepper. Add sausage mixture along with the remaining Spanish Red Beans & Rice with Sausage Mix. Stir to incorporate. Continue cooking on high for another 1 1/2 hours, stirring occasionally.

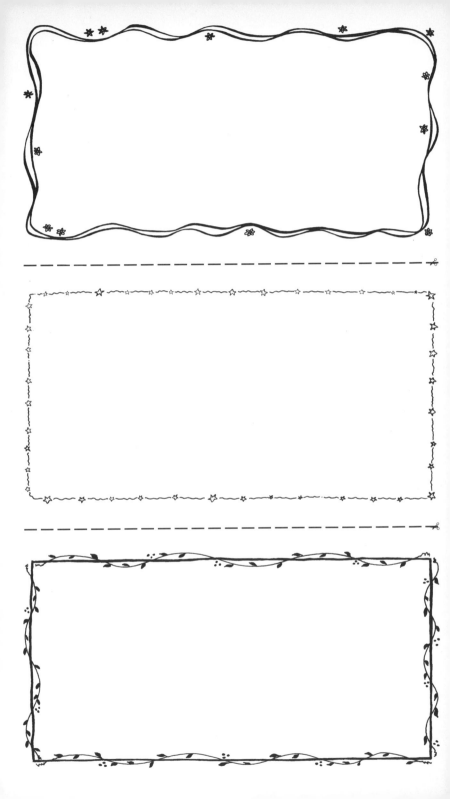

Apple Pecan Pudding Cake Mix

1 C. sugar
3/4 C. chopped pecans
3/4 C. brown sugar
1 1/2 tsp. baking soda
1/2 tsp. salt
3/4 tsp. nutmeg
1 1/2 tsp. cinnamon
1 3/4 C. flour

Layer the ingredients in the order given into a wide-mouth 1-quart canning jar. Pack each layer into place before adding the next ingredient.

Attach a gift tag with the mixing and cooking instructions.

Apple Pecan Pudding Cake

1 jar Apple Pecan Pudding
  Cake Mix
2 eggs
2 tsp. vanilla
1 C. vegetable oil
2 C. peeled & diced apples

Empty contents of jar into a large mixing bowl, stirring to combine. Add eggs, vanilla, oil and apples. Beat until well combined. Place greased bread pan or greased tin cans (any heat proof mold that will fit) into slow cooker, filling cake containers 2/3 full. Cook on high for 3 1/2 to 4 hours.

Apple Pecan Pudding Cake

1 jar Apple Pecan Pudding
   Cake Mix
2 eggs

2 tsp. vanilla
1 C. vegetable oil
2 C. peeled & diced apples

    Empty contents of jar into a large mixing bowl, stirring to combine. Add eggs, vanilla, oil and apples. Beat until well combined. Place greased bread pan or greased tin cans (any heat proof mold that will fit) into slow cooker, filling cake containers 2/3 full. Cook on high for 3 1/2 to 4 hours.

Apple Pecan Pudding Cake

1 jar Apple Pecan Pudding
   Cake Mix
2 eggs

2 tsp. vanilla
1 C. vegetable oil
2 C. peeled & diced apples

    Empty contents of jar into a large mixing bowl, stirring to combine. Add eggs, vanilla, oil and apples. Beat until well combined. Place greased bread pan or greased tin cans (any heat proof mold that will fit) into slow cooker, filling cake containers 2/3 full. Cook on high for 3 1/2 to 4 hours.

Apple Pecan Pudding Cake

1 jar Apple Pecan Pudding
   Cake Mix
2 eggs

2 tsp. vanilla
1 C. vegetable oil
2 C. peeled & diced apples

    Empty contents of jar into a large mixing bowl, stirring to combine. Add eggs, vanilla, oil and apples. Beat until well combined. Place greased bread pan or greased tin cans (any heat proof mold that will fit) into slow cooker, filling cake containers 2/3 full. Cook on high for 3 1/2 to 4 hours.

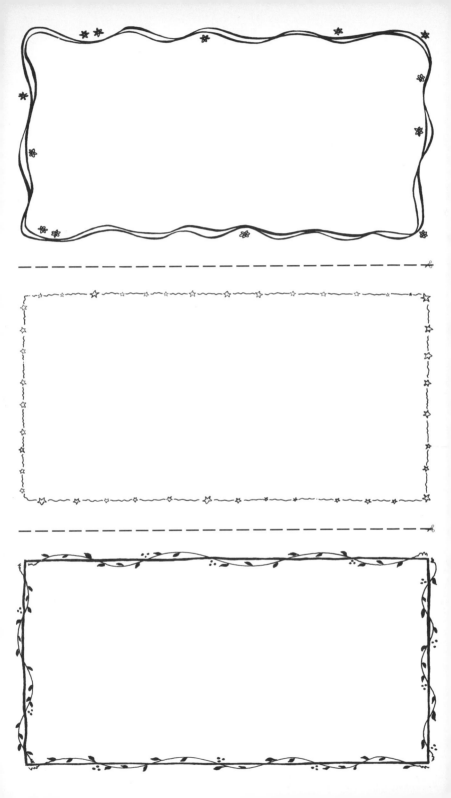

Apple Pecan Pudding Cake

1 jar Apple Pecan Pudding
  Cake Mix
2 eggs

2 tsp. vanilla
1 C. vegetable oil
2 C. peeled & diced apples

    Empty contents of jar into a large mixing bowl, stirring to combine. Add eggs, vanilla, oil and apples. Beat until well combined. Place greased bread pan or greased tin cans (any heat proof mold that will fit) into slow cooker, filling cake containers 2/3 full. Cook on high for 3 1/2 to 4 hours.

Apple Pecan Pudding Cake

1 jar Apple Pecan Pudding
  Cake Mix
2 eggs

2 tsp. vanilla
1 C. vegetable oil
2 C. peeled & diced apples

    Empty contents of jar into a large mixing bowl, stirring to combine. Add eggs, vanilla, oil and apples. Beat until well combined. Place greased bread pan or greased tin cans (any heat proof mold that will fit) into slow cooker, filling cake containers 2/3 full. Cook on high for 3 1/2 to 4 hours.

Apple Pecan Pudding Cake

1 jar Apple Pecan Pudding
  Cake Mix
2 eggs

2 tsp. vanilla
1 C. vegetable oil
2 C. peeled & diced apples

    Empty contents of jar into a large mixing bowl, stirring to combine. Add eggs, vanilla, oil and apples. Beat until well combined. Place greased bread pan or greased tin cans (any heat proof mold that will fit) into slow cooker, filling cake containers 2/3 full. Cook on high for 3 1/2 to 4 hours.

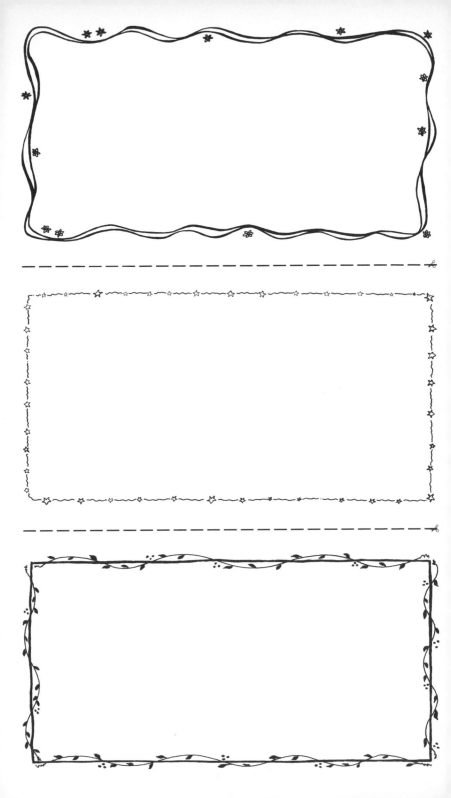

Tuna Noodle Casserole Mix

1 T. dried minced onions
2 T. dried celery flakes
1 T. dried parsley
1 pkg. Knorr® White Sauce
3/4 C. Parmesan cheese
3 C. medium egg noodles

Layer the ingredients in the order given into a wide-mouth 1-quart canning jar. Pack each layer in place before adding the next ingredient.

Attach a gift tag with the cooking instructions.

❀ A half-yard of fabric should make eight wide-mouth jar covers. ❀

Tuna Noodle Casserole

1 jar Tuna Noodle Casserole Mix
4 1/4 C. whole milk
1/3 C. butter
1 can tuna, drained

Empty contents of jar into slow cooker, stirring to combine. In a saucepan, bring milk and butter to a boil. Pour milk and butter mixture over dry ingredients, stirring with a whisk to fully incorporate sauce. Stir in tuna. Cook on high for 1 1/2 to 2 hours.

Tuna Noodle Casserole

1 jar Tuna Noodle Casserole Mix   1/3 C. butter
4 1/4 C. whole milk   1 can tuna, drained

Empty contents of jar into slow cooker, stirring to combine. In a saucepan, bring milk and butter to a boil. Pour milk and butter mixture over dry ingredients, stirring with a whisk to fully incorporate sauce. Stir in tuna. Cook on high for 1 1/2 to 2 hours.

Tuna Noodle Casserole

1 jar Tuna Noodle Casserole Mix   1/3 C. butter
4 1/4 C. whole milk   1 can tuna, drained

Empty contents of jar into slow cooker, stirring to combine. In a saucepan, bring milk and butter to a boil. Pour milk and butter mixture over dry ingredients, stirring with a whisk to fully incorporate sauce. Stir in tuna. Cook on high for 1 1/2 to 2 hours.

Tuna Noodle Casserole

1 jar Tuna Noodle Casserole Mix   1/3 C. butter
4 1/4 C. whole milk   1 can tuna, drained

Empty contents of jar into slow cooker, stirring to combine. In a saucepan, bring milk and butter to a boil. Pour milk and butter mixture over dry ingredients, stirring with a whisk to fully incorporate sauce. Stir in tuna. Cook on high for 1 1/2 to 2 hours.

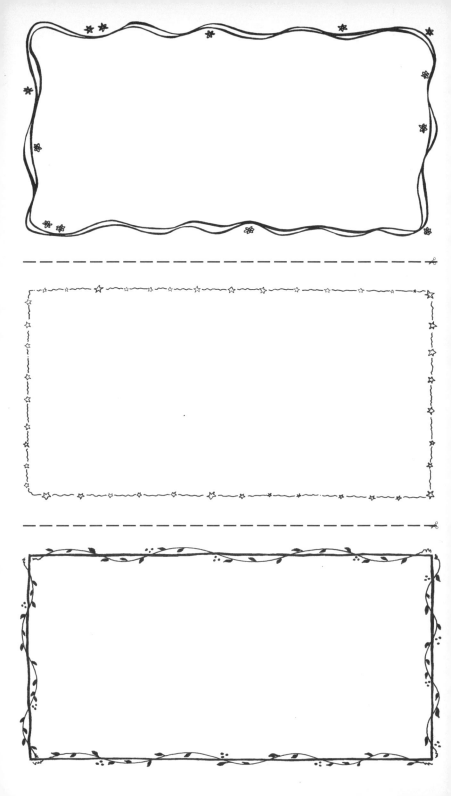

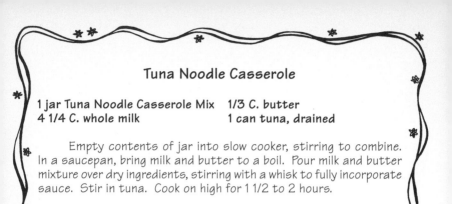

Tuna Noodle Casserole

1 jar Tuna Noodle Casserole Mix   1/3 C. butter
4 1/4 C. whole milk   1 can tuna, drained

    Empty contents of jar into slow cooker, stirring to combine. In a saucepan, bring milk and butter to a boil. Pour milk and butter mixture over dry ingredients, stirring with a whisk to fully incorporate sauce. Stir in tuna. Cook on high for 1 1/2 to 2 hours.

Tuna Noodle Casserole

1 jar Tuna Noodle Casserole Mix   1/3 C. butter
4 1/4 C. whole milk   1 can tuna, drained

    Empty contents of jar into slow cooker, stirring to combine. In a saucepan, bring milk and butter to a boil. Pour milk and butter mixture over dry ingredients, stirring with a whisk to fully incorporate sauce. Stir in tuna. Cook on high for 1 1/2 to 2 hours.

Tuna Noodle Casserole

1 jar Tuna Noodle Casserole Mix   1/3 C. butter
4 1/4 C. whole milk   1 can tuna, drained

    Empty contents of jar into slow cooker, stirring to combine. In a saucepan, bring milk and butter to a boil. Pour milk and butter mixture over dry ingredients, stirring with a whisk to fully incorporate sauce. Stir in tuna. Cook on high for 1 1/2 to 2 hours.

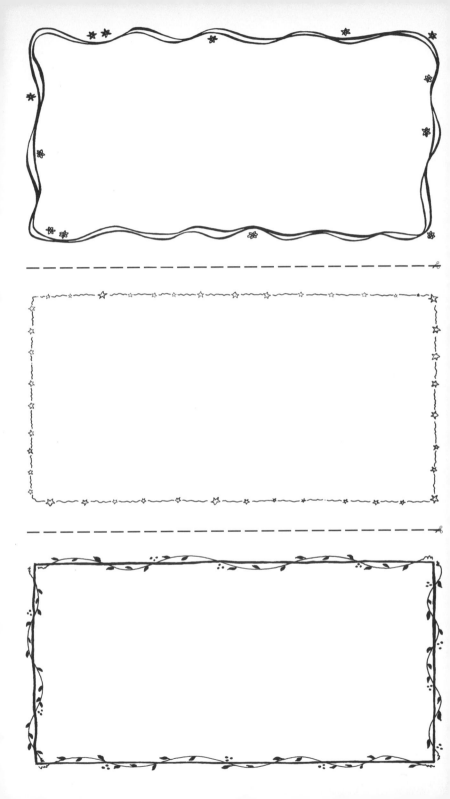

Chocolate Bread Pudding Mix

1/4 C. cocoa powder (clean
    inside of jar with a paper towel
    after this layer)
1/4 tsp. cinnamon
1/2 C. sugar
3/4 C. semi-sweet chocolate
    chips
3 C. store-bought unseasoned
    dried bread cubes

Layer the ingredients in the order given into a wide-mouth 1-quart canning jar. Pack each layer into place before adding the next ingredient.

Attach a gift tag with the mixing and cooking instructions.

Chocolate Bread Pudding

1 jar Chocolate Bread Pudding
  Mix
1 Qt. whole milk
2 eggs
2 tsp. vanilla

Butter bottom and sides of slow cooker. Empty jar contents into crock, stirring to combine. In a saucepan, bring milk to a simmer then pour over dry ingredients. Let sit for 10 minutes allowing milk to cool, chocolate to partially melt and bread to absorb liquid. Whisk together eggs and vanilla and stir into bread mixture until fully incorporated. Cook on high for 1 1/2 to 2 hours.

Chocolate Bread Pudding

| 1 jar Chocolate Bread Pudding Mix | 2 eggs |
| 1 Qt. whole milk | 2 tsp. vanilla |

Butter bottom and sides of slow cooker. Empty jar contents into crock, stirring to combine. In a saucepan, bring milk to a simmer then pour over dry ingredients. Let sit for 10 minutes allowing milk to cool, chocolate to partially melt and bread to absorb liquid. Whisk together eggs and vanilla and stir into bread mixture until fully incorporated. Cook on high for 1 1/2 to 2 hours.

- ✂

Chocolate Bread Pudding

| 1 jar Chocolate Bread Pudding Mix | 2 eggs |
| 1 Qt. whole milk | 2 tsp. vanilla |

Butter bottom and sides of slow cooker. Empty jar contents into crock, stirring to combine. In a saucepan, bring milk to a simmer then pour over dry ingredients. Let sit for 10 minutes allowing milk to cool, chocolate to partially melt and bread to absorb liquid. Whisk together eggs and vanilla and stir into bread mixture until fully incorporated. Cook on high for 1 1/2 to 2 hours.

- ✂

Chocolate Bread Pudding

| 1 jar Chocolate Bread Pudding Mix | 2 eggs |
| 1 Qt. whole milk | 2 tsp. vanilla |

Butter bottom and sides of slow cooker. Empty jar contents into crock, stirring to combine. In a saucepan, bring milk to a simmer then pour over dry ingredients. Let sit for 10 minutes allowing milk to cool, chocolate to partially melt and bread to absorb liquid. Whisk together eggs and vanilla and stir into bread mixture until fully incorporated. Cook on high for 1 1/2 to 2 hours.

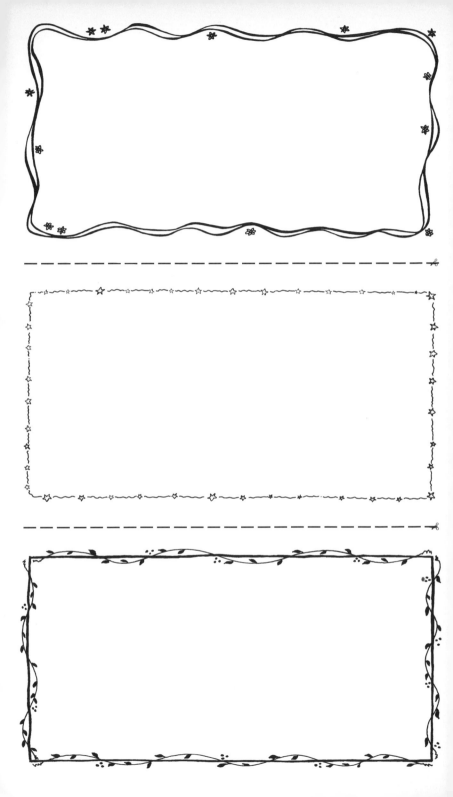

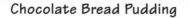

Chocolate Bread Pudding

1 jar Chocolate Bread Pudding Mix
1 Qt. whole milk

2 eggs
2 tsp. vanilla

    Butter bottom and sides of slow cooker. Empty jar contents into crock, stirring to combine. In a saucepan, bring milk to a simmer then pour over dry ingredients. Let sit for 10 minutes allowing milk to cool, chocolate to partially melt and bread to absorb liquid. Whisk together eggs and vanilla and stir into bread mixture until fully incorporated. Cook on high for 1 1/2 to 2 hours.

Chocolate Bread Pudding

1 jar Chocolate Bread Pudding Mix
1 Qt. whole milk

2 eggs
2 tsp. vanilla

    Butter bottom and sides of slow cooker. Empty jar contents into crock, stirring to combine. In a saucepan, bring milk to a simmer then pour over dry ingredients. Let sit for 10 minutes allowing milk to cool, chocolate to partially melt and bread to absorb liquid. Whisk together eggs and vanilla and stir into bread mixture until fully incorporated. Cook on high for 1 1/2 to 2 hours.

Chocolate Bread Pudding

1 jar Chocolate Bread Pudding Mix
1 Qt. whole milk

2 eggs
2 tsp. vanilla

    Butter bottom and sides of slow cooker. Empty jar contents into crock, stirring to combine. In a saucepan, bring milk to a simmer then pour over dry ingredients. Let sit for 10 minutes allowing milk to cool, chocolate to partially melt and bread to absorb liquid. Whisk together eggs and vanilla and stir into bread mixture until fully incorporated. Cook on high for 1 1/2 to 2 hours.

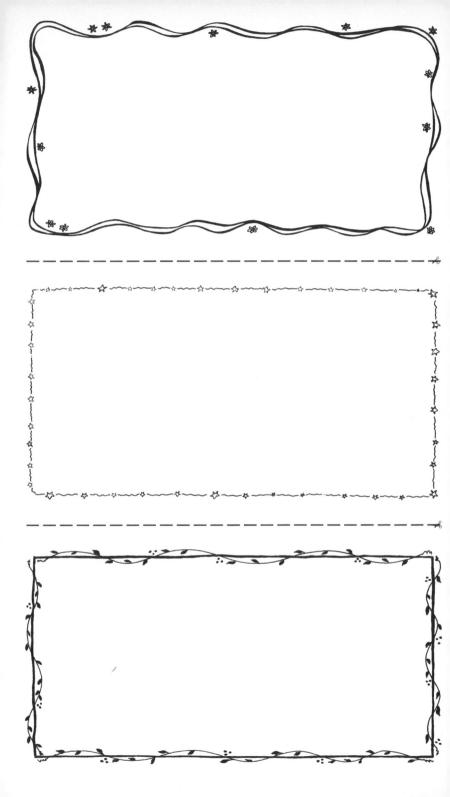

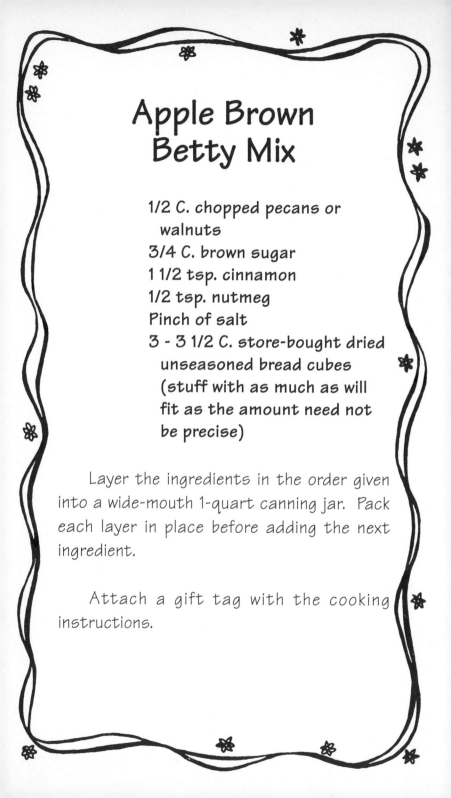

Apple Brown Betty Mix

1/2 C. chopped pecans or
   walnuts
3/4 C. brown sugar
1 1/2 tsp. cinnamon
1/2 tsp. nutmeg
Pinch of salt
3 - 3 1/2 C. store-bought dried
   unseasoned bread cubes
   (stuff with as much as will
   fit as the amount need not
   be precise)

Layer the ingredients in the order given into a wide-mouth 1-quart canning jar. Pack each layer in place before adding the next ingredient.

Attach a gift tag with the cooking instructions.

Apple Brown Betty

1 jar Apple Brown Betty Mix
5 -6 tart apples
1/2 C. butter or margarine
1/4 C. milk
Ice cream or whipped cream,
   optional

Butter bottom and sides of slow cooker. Peel, core and cut apples into eighths. Place apples over bottom of crock. In a saucepan, melt butter with milk. Empty contents of jar into a large bowl and toss with butter and milk mixture. Place on top of apples. Cook on low for 3 to 4 hours or on high for 2 hours. If desired, serve with ice cream or whipped cream.

Apple Brown Betty

1 jar Apple Brown Betty Mix
5 -6 tart apples
1/2 C. butter or margarine

1/4 C. milk
Ice cream or whipped
  cream, optional

  Butter bottom and sides of slow cooker. Peel, core and cut apples into eighths. Place apples over bottom of crock. In a saucepan, melt butter with milk. Empty contents of jar into a large bowl and toss with butter and milk mixture. Place on top of apples. Cook on low for 3 to 4 hours or on high for 2 hours. If desired, serve with ice cream or whipped cream.

Apple Brown Betty

1 jar Apple Brown Betty Mix
5 -6 tart apples
1/2 C. butter or margarine

1/4 C. milk
Ice cream or whipped
  cream, optional

  Butter bottom and sides of slow cooker. Peel, core and cut apples into eighths. Place apples over bottom of crock. In a saucepan, melt butter with milk. Empty contents of jar into a large bowl and toss with butter and milk mixture. Place on top of apples. Cook on low for 3 to 4 hours or on high for 2 hours. If desired, serve with ice cream or whipped cream.

Apple Brown Betty

1 jar Apple Brown Betty Mix
5 -6 tart apples
1/2 C. butter or margarine

1/4 C. milk
Ice cream or whipped
  cream, optional

  Butter bottom and sides of slow cooker. Peel, core and cut apples into eighths. Place apples over bottom of crock. In a saucepan, melt butter with milk. Empty contents of jar into a large bowl and toss with butter and milk mixture. Place on top of apples. Cook on low for 3 to 4 hours or on high for 2 hours. If desired, serve with ice cream or whipped cream.

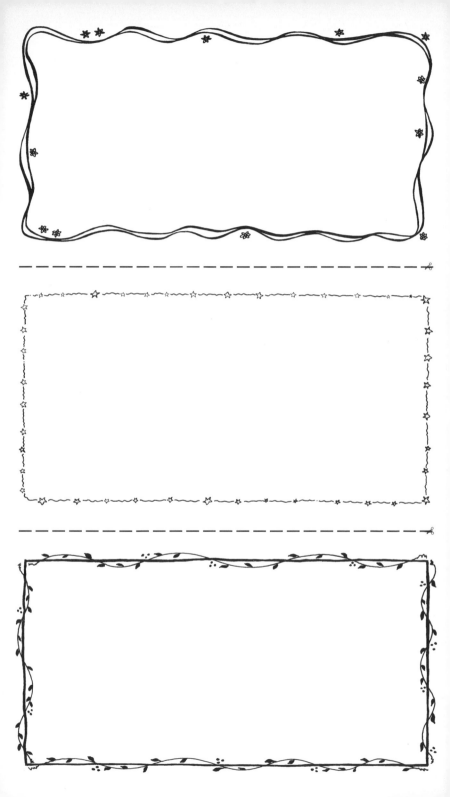

Apple Brown Betty

1 jar Apple Brown Betty Mix
5 -6 tart apples
1/2 C. butter or margarine

1/4 C. milk
Ice cream or whipped
   cream, optional

    Butter bottom and sides of slow cooker. Peel, core and cut apples into eighths. Place apples over bottom of crock. In a saucepan, melt butter with milk. Empty contents of jar into a large bowl and toss with butter and milk mixture. Place on top of apples. Cook on low for 3 to 4 hours or on high for 2 hours. If desired, serve with ice cream or whipped cream.

Apple Brown Betty

1 jar Apple Brown Betty Mix
5 -6 tart apples
1/2 C. butter or margarine

1/4 C. milk
Ice cream or whipped
   cream, optional

    Butter bottom and sides of slow cooker. Peel, core and cut apples into eighths. Place apples over bottom of crock. In a saucepan, melt butter with milk. Empty contents of jar into a large bowl and toss with butter and milk mixture. Place on top of apples. Cook on low for 3 to 4 hours or on high for 2 hours. If desired, serve with ice cream or whipped cream.

Apple Brown Betty

1 jar Apple Brown Betty Mix
5 -6 tart apples
1/2 C. butter or margarine

1/4 C. milk
Ice cream or whipped
   cream, optional

    Butter bottom and sides of slow cooker. Peel, core and cut apples into eighths. Place apples over bottom of crock. In a saucepan, melt butter with milk. Empty contents of jar into a large bowl and toss with butter and milk mixture. Place on top of apples. Cook on low for 3 to 4 hours or on high for 2 hours. If desired, serve with ice cream or whipped cream.

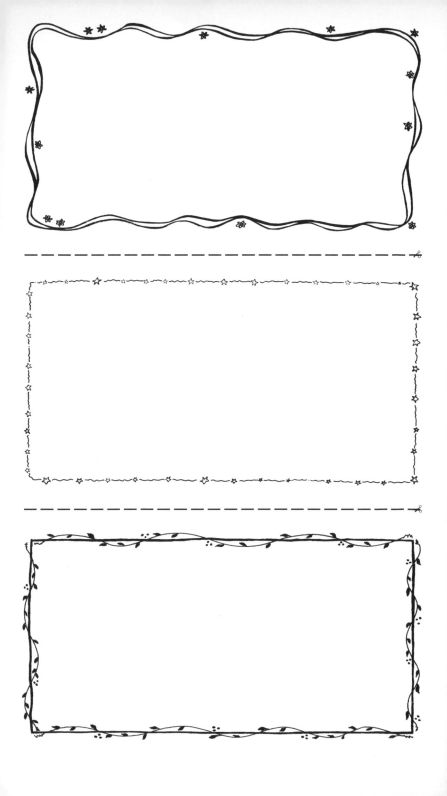

Black Bean Chili Mix

Seasoning Packet:
2 T. chili powder
1 tsp. cumin
1 tsp. garlic powder
2 T. dried minced onion
2 T. beef bouillon

1 bay leaf (place down the side
   of the jar)
3 3/4 C. black beans

Mix and place the seasonings in a small plastic bag. Place the packet into a wide-mouth 1-quart canning jar. Add the bay leaf and black beans.

Attach a gift tag with the cooking instructions.

❀ *To spice up certain Gifts in a Jar dishes, attach a small bottle of Tabasco sauce to the jars.* ❀

Black Bean Chili

1 jar Black Bean Chili Mix
2 lbs. ground beef or cubed
 stew beef
1 (29 oz.) can diced tomatoes
 with juice

Remove beans from Black Bean Chili Mix. Wash beans then place in a microwave safe dish, filling with water 1 to 1 1/2 inches over the beans. Cover tightly with plastic wrap, poking three small holes in the top with a sharp knife. Microwave on high for 9 minutes, rotate and microwave for another 9 minutes. Drain beans, and place in slow cooker. Cover with 8 cups hot water, turning slow cooker on high. In a sauté pan, brown beef, drain fat then add to crock. Add seasoning packet, tomatoes and bay leaf. Cook on high for 5 to 6 hours or on low for 8 to 10 hours. Remove and discard bay leaf.

Black Bean Chili

1 jar Black Bean Chili Mix
2 lbs. ground beef or cubed
   stew beef

1 (29 oz.) can diced tomatoes
   with juice

    Remove beans from Black Bean Chili Mix. Wash beans then place in a microwave safe dish, filling with water 1 to 1 1/2 inches over the beans. Cover tightly with plastic wrap, poking three small holes in the top with a sharp knife. Microwave on high for 9 minutes, rotate and microwave for another 9 minutes. Drain beans, and place in slow cooker. Cover with 8 cups hot water, turning slow cooker on high. In a sauté pan, brown beef, drain fat then add to crock. Add seasoning packet, tomatoes and bay leaf. Cook on high for 5 to 6 hours or on low for 8 to 10 hours. Remove and discard bay leaf.

Black Bean Chili

1 jar Black Bean Chili Mix
2 lbs. ground beef or cubed
   stew beef

1 (29 oz.) can diced tomatoes
   with juice

    Remove beans from Black Bean Chili Mix. Wash beans then place in a microwave safe dish, filling with water 1 to 1 1/2 inches over the beans. Cover tightly with plastic wrap, poking three small holes in the top with a sharp knife. Microwave on high for 9 minutes, rotate and microwave for another 9 minutes. Drain beans, and place in slow cooker. Cover with 8 cups hot water, turning slow cooker on high. In a sauté pan, brown beef, drain fat then add to crock. Add seasoning packet, tomatoes and bay leaf. Cook on high for 5 to 6 hours or on low for 8 to 10 hours. Remove and discard bay leaf.

Black Bean Chili

1 jar Black Bean Chili Mix
2 lbs. ground beef or cubed
   stew beef

1 (29 oz.) can diced tomatoes
   with juice

    Remove beans from Black Bean Chili Mix. Wash beans then place in a microwave safe dish, filling with water 1 to 1 1/2 inches over the beans. Cover tightly with plastic wrap, poking three small holes in the top with a sharp knife. Microwave on high for 9 minutes, rotate and microwave for another 9 minutes. Drain beans, and place in slow cooker. Cover with 8 cups hot water, turning slow cooker on high. In a sauté pan, brown beef, drain fat then add to crock. Add seasoning packet, tomatoes and bay leaf. Cook on high for 5 to 6 hours or on low for 8 to 10 hours. Remove and discard bay leaf.

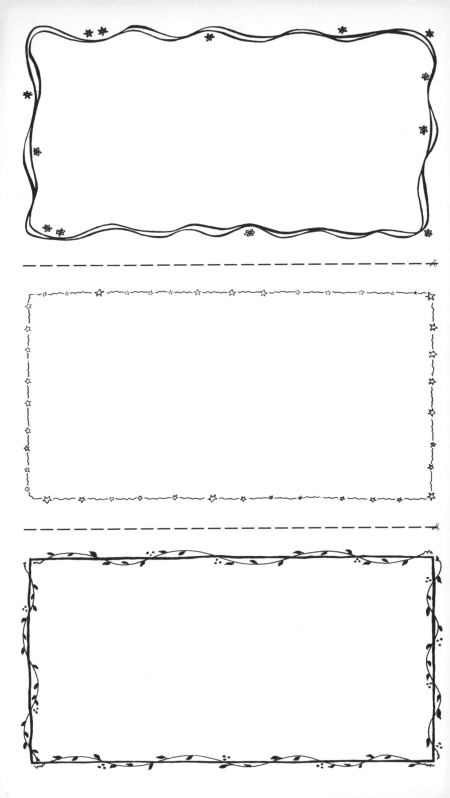

Black Bean Chili

1 jar Black Bean Chili Mix
2 lbs. ground beef or cubed
   stew beef

1 (29 oz.) can diced tomatoes
   with juice

    Remove beans from Black Bean Chili Mix. Wash beans then place in a microwave safe dish, filling with water 1 to 1 1/2 inches over the beans. Cover tightly with plastic wrap, poking three small holes in the top with a sharp knife. Microwave on high for 9 minutes, rotate and microwave for another 9 minutes. Drain beans, and place in slow cooker. Cover with 8 cups hot water, turning slow cooker on high. In a sauté pan, brown beef, drain fat then add to crock. Add seasoning packet, tomatoes and bay leaf. Cook on high for 5 to 6 hours or on low for 8 to 10 hours. Remove and discard bay leaf.

- ✂

Black Bean Chili

1 jar Black Bean Chili Mix
2 lbs. ground beef or cubed
   stew beef

1 (29 oz.) can diced tomatoes
   with juice

    Remove beans from Black Bean Chili Mix. Wash beans then place in a microwave safe dish, filling with water 1 to 1 1/2 inches over the beans. Cover tightly with plastic wrap, poking three small holes in the top with a sharp knife. Microwave on high for 9 minutes, rotate and microwave for another 9 minutes. Drain beans, and place in slow cooker. Cover with 8 cups hot water, turning slow cooker on high. In a sauté pan, brown beef, drain fat then add to crock. Add seasoning packet, tomatoes and bay leaf. Cook on high for 5 to 6 hours or on low for 8 to 10 hours. Remove and discard bay leaf.

- ✂

Black Bean Chili

1 jar Black Bean Chili Mix
2 lbs. ground beef or cubed
   stew beef

1 (29 oz.) can diced tomatoes
   with juice

    Remove beans from Black Bean Chili Mix. Wash beans then place in a microwave safe dish, filling with water 1 to 1 1/2 inches over the beans. Cover tightly with plastic wrap, poking three small holes in the top with a sharp knife. Microwave on high for 9 minutes, rotate and microwave for another 9 minutes. Drain beans, and place in slow cooker. Cover with 8 cups hot water, turning slow cooker on high. In a sauté pan, brown beef, drain fat then add to crock. Add seasoning packet, tomatoes and bay leaf. Cook on high for 5 to 6 hours or on low for 8 to 10 hours. Remove and discard bay leaf.

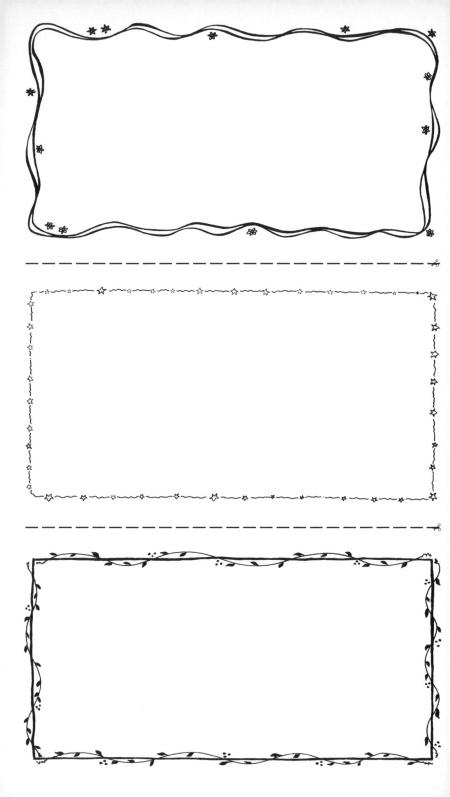

Peach Pie Coffee Cake Mix

1 C. flour
1/2 C. sliced almonds, toasted
   and cooled completely*
1/2 C. brown sugar
1 1/4 C. flour
1 tsp. salt
1 1/2 tsp. baking powder
1 tsp. baking soda

1 C. sugar in a baggie

Layer the ingredients in the order given into a wide-mouth 1-quart canning jar. Pack each layer into place before adding the next ingredient. Place sugar on top of the baking soda.

Attach a gift tag with the mixing and cooking instructions.

*To toast almonds, place nuts in a single layer on a baking sheet. Bake at 350°F for approximately 10 minutes or until nuts are golden brown.

Peach Pie Coffee Cake

1 jar Peach Pie Coffee Cake Mix
6 T. butter or margarine
2 eggs
1 1/4 C. sour cream
1 tsp. vanilla
1/2 tsp. almond extract
1 (20 oz.) can peach pie filling

In a mixing bowl, beat sugar from baggie and butter on high speed until lightened in color and texture. Beat eggs into mixture one at a time. In a small bowl, combine sour cream, vanilla and almond extract. Add jar ingredients and sour cream mixture to sugar mixture half at a time, beating on low speed until smooth. Butter the bottom and sides of slow cooker. Spread peach pie filling over the bottom of the crock. Place batter over pie filling. Cook on high for 2 to 2 1/2 hours. Invert cake onto a serving tray.

Peach Pie Coffee Cake

1 jar Peach Pie Coffee Cake Mix
6 T. butter or margarine
2 eggs
1 1/4 C. sour cream
1 tsp. vanilla
1/2 tsp. almond extract
1 (20 oz.) can peach pie filling

In a mixing bowl, beat sugar from baggie and butter on high speed until lightened in color and texture. Beat eggs into mixture one at a time. In a small bowl, combine sour cream, vanilla and almond extract. Add jar ingredients and sour cream mixture to sugar mixture half at a time, beating on low speed until smooth. Butter the bottom and sides of slow cooker. Spread peach pie filling over the bottom of the crock. Place batter over pie filling. Cook on high for 2 to 2 1/2 hours. Invert cake onto a serving tray.

Peach Pie Coffee Cake

1 jar Peach Pie Coffee Cake Mix
6 T. butter or margarine
2 eggs
1 1/4 C. sour cream
1 tsp. vanilla
1/2 tsp. almond extract
1 (20 oz.) can peach pie filling

In a mixing bowl, beat sugar from baggie and butter on high speed until lightened in color and texture. Beat eggs into mixture one at a time. In a small bowl, combine sour cream, vanilla and almond extract. Add jar ingredients and sour cream mixture to sugar mixture half at a time, beating on low speed until smooth. Butter the bottom and sides of slow cooker. Spread peach pie filling over the bottom of the crock. Place batter over pie filling. Cook on high for 2 to 2 1/2 hours. Invert cake onto a serving tray.

Peach Pie Coffee Cake

1 jar Peach Pie Coffee Cake Mix
6 T. butter or margarine
2 eggs
1 1/4 C. sour cream
1 tsp. vanilla
1/2 tsp. almond extract
1 (20 oz.) can peach pie filling

In a mixing bowl, beat sugar from baggie and butter on high speed until lightened in color and texture. Beat eggs into mixture one at a time. In a small bowl, combine sour cream, vanilla and almond extract. Add jar ingredients and sour cream mixture to sugar mixture half at a time, beating on low speed until smooth. Butter the bottom and sides of slow cooker. Spread peach pie filling over the bottom of the crock. Place batter over pie filling. Cook on high for 2 to 2 1/2 hours. Invert cake onto a serving tray.

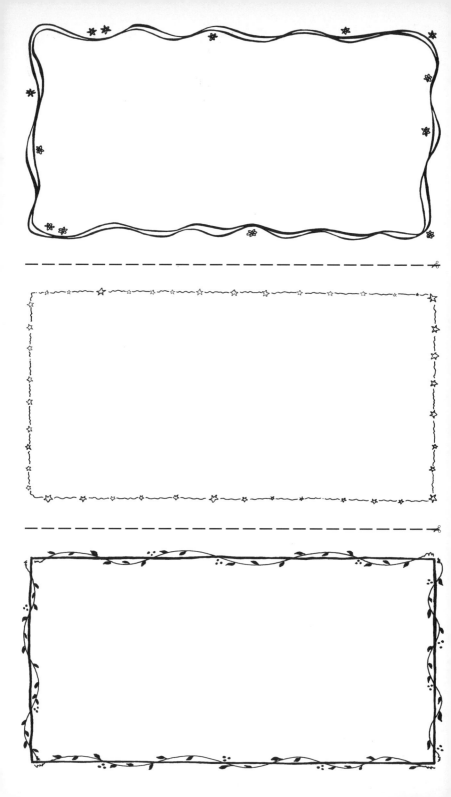

Peach Pie Coffee Cake

1 jar Peach Pie Coffee Cake Mix
6 T. butter or margarine
2 eggs
1 1/4 C. sour cream

1 tsp. vanilla
1/2 tsp. almond extract
1 (20 oz.) can peach pie filling

In a mixing bowl, beat sugar from baggie and butter on high speed until lightened in color and texture. Beat eggs into mixture one at a time. In a small bowl, combine sour cream, vanilla and almond extract. Add jar ingredients and sour cream mixture to sugar mixture half at a time, beating on low speed until smooth. Butter the bottom and sides of slow cooker. Spread peach pie filling over the bottom of the crock. Place batter over pie filling. Cook on high for 2 to 2 1/2 hours. Invert cake onto a serving tray.

Peach Pie Coffee Cake

1 jar Peach Pie Coffee Cake Mix
6 T. butter or margarine
2 eggs
1 1/4 C. sour cream

1 tsp. vanilla
1/2 tsp. almond extract
1 (20 oz.) can peach pie filling

In a mixing bowl, beat sugar from baggie and butter on high speed until lightened in color and texture. Beat eggs into mixture one at a time. In a small bowl, combine sour cream, vanilla and almond extract. Add jar ingredients and sour cream mixture to sugar mixture half at a time, beating on low speed until smooth. Butter the bottom and sides of slow cooker. Spread peach pie filling over the bottom of the crock. Place batter over pie filling. Cook on high for 2 to 2 1/2 hours. Invert cake onto a serving tray.

Peach Pie Coffee Cake

1 jar Peach Pie Coffee Cake Mix
6 T. butter or margarine
2 eggs
1 1/4 C. sour cream

1 tsp. vanilla
1/2 tsp. almond extract
1 (20 oz.) can peach pie filling

In a mixing bowl, beat sugar from baggie and butter on high speed until lightened in color and texture. Beat eggs into mixture one at a time. In a small bowl, combine sour cream, vanilla and almond extract. Add jar ingredients and sour cream mixture to sugar mixture half at a time, beating on low speed until smooth. Butter the bottom and sides of slow cooker. Spread peach pie filling over the bottom of the crock. Place batter over pie filling. Cook on high for 2 to 2 1/2 hours. Invert cake onto a serving tray.

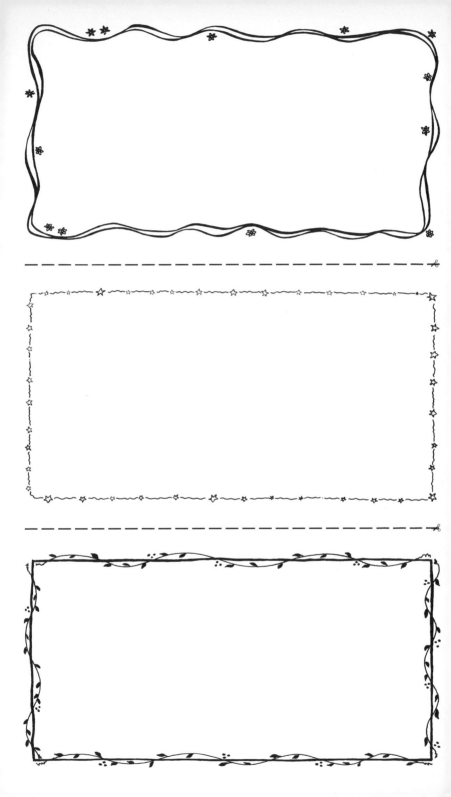

Spanish Noodle & Beef Casserole Mix

1 T. chili powder
2 T. dried minced onion
1/2 T. dried minced garlic
3 T. real bacon bits
3 3/4 C. medium egg noodles

Layer the ingredients in the order given into a wide-mouth 1-quart canning jar. Pack each layer into place before adding the next ingredient.

Attach a gift tag with the cooking instructions.

❀ *For a different look, place a small amount of stuffing under a fabric cover before attaching to "puff" the top.* ❀

Spanish Noodle & Beef Casserole

1 jar Spanish Noodle & Beef
  Casserole Mix
1 (14 oz.) can diced tomatoes
  with juice
1 lb. ground beef
1 medium green pepper, diced

Empty contents of jar into slow cooker, stirring to combine. In a saucepan, bring 2 cups water to a boil. Pour over dry ingredients. Stir in tomatoes. In a sauté pan, brown ground beef and green pepper. Drain fat and stir into casserole. Cook on high for 1 1/2 to 2 hours.

Spanish Noodle & Beef Casserole

1 jar Spanish Noodle & Beef
  Casserole Mix
1 (14 oz.) can diced tomatoes
  with juice

1 lb. ground beef
1 medium green pepper, diced

Empty contents of jar into slow cooker, stirring to combine. In a saucepan, bring 2 cups water to a boil. Pour over dry ingredients. Stir in tomatoes. In a sauté pan, brown ground beef and green pepper. Drain fat and stir into casserole. Cook on high for 1 1/2 to 2 hours.

Spanish Noodle & Beef Casserole

1 jar Spanish Noodle & Beef
  Casserole Mix
1 (14 oz.) can diced tomatoes
  with juice

1 lb. ground beef
1 medium green pepper, diced

Empty contents of jar into slow cooker, stirring to combine. In a saucepan, bring 2 cups water to a boil. Pour over dry ingredients. Stir in tomatoes. In a sauté pan, brown ground beef and green pepper. Drain fat and stir into casserole. Cook on high for 1 1/2 to 2 hours.

Spanish Noodle & Beef Casserole

1 jar Spanish Noodle & Beef
  Casserole Mix
1 (14 oz.) can diced tomatoes
  with juice

1 lb. ground beef
1 medium green pepper, diced

Empty contents of jar into slow cooker, stirring to combine. In a saucepan, bring 2 cups water to a boil. Pour over dry ingredients. Stir in tomatoes. In a sauté pan, brown ground beef and green pepper. Drain fat and stir into casserole. Cook on high for 1 1/2 to 2 hours.

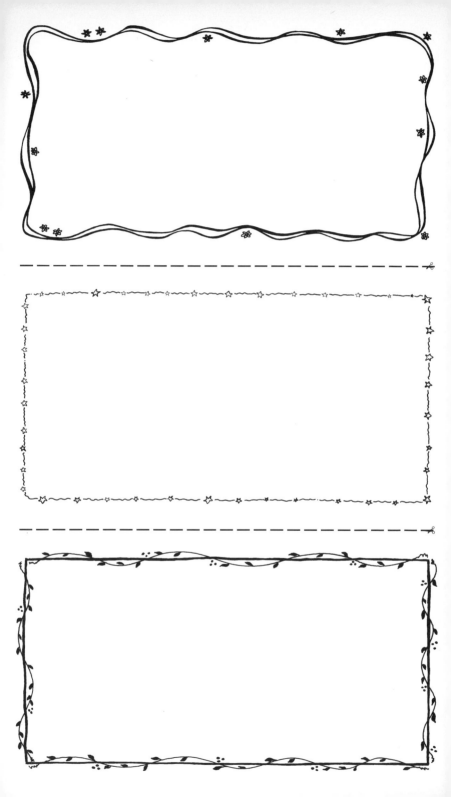

Spanish Noodle & Beef Casserole

1 jar Spanish Noodle & Beef
  Casserole Mix
1 (14 oz.) can diced tomatoes
  with juice

1 lb. ground beef
1 medium green pepper, diced

    Empty contents of jar into slow cooker, stirring to combine.
In a saucepan, bring 2 cups water to a boil. Pour over dry ingredients.
Stir in tomatoes. In a sauté pan, brown ground beef and green pepper.
Drain fat and stir into casserole. Cook on high for 1 1/2 to 2 hours.

Spanish Noodle & Beef Casserole

1 jar Spanish Noodle & Beef
  Casserole Mix
1 (14 oz.) can diced tomatoes
  with juice

1 lb. ground beef
1 medium green pepper, diced

    Empty contents of jar into slow cooker, stirring to combine.
In a saucepan, bring 2 cups water to a boil. Pour over dry ingredients.
Stir in tomatoes. In a sauté pan, brown ground beef and green pepper.
Drain fat and stir into casserole. Cook on high for 1 1/2 to 2 hours.

Spanish Noodle & Beef Casserole

1 jar Spanish Noodle & Beef
  Casserole Mix
1 (14 oz.) can diced tomatoes
  with juice

1 lb. ground beef
1 medium green pepper, diced

    Empty contents of jar into slow cooker, stirring to combine.
In a saucepan, bring 2 cups water to a boil. Pour over dry ingredients.
Stir in tomatoes. In a sauté pan, brown ground beef and green pepper.
Drain fat and stir into casserole. Cook on high for 1 1/2 to 2 hours.

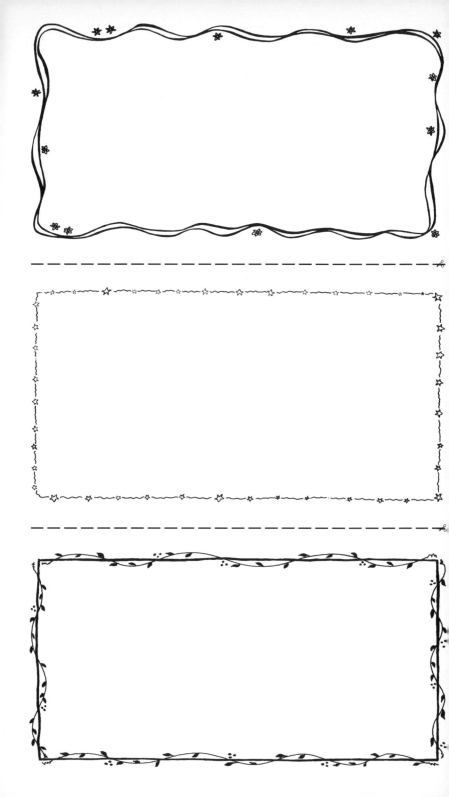

Chicken & Rice Casserole Mix

3/4 C. powdered coffee creamer
1 (1 oz.) pkg. Hidden Valley
   Ranch dressing mix
1/2 C. Parmesan cheese
3/4 C. sliced almonds, toasted
   and cooled completely*
1/4 C. real bacon bits
1 3/4 C. white rice

Layer the ingredients in the order given into a wide-mouth 1-quart canning jar. Pack each layer into place before adding the next ingredient.

Attach a gift tag with the cooking instructions.

*To toast almonds, place nuts in a single layer on a baking sheet. Bake at 350°F for approximately 10 minutes or until nuts are golden brown.

Chicken & Rice Casserole

1 jar Chicken & Rice
 Casserole Mix
1 - 1 1/2 lbs. chicken breast,
 diced

Empty contents of jar into slow cooker, stirring to combine. In a saucepan, bring 4 1/2 cups water to a boil. Pour water over rice mixture and stir. In a sauté pan, brown chicken. Add to crock and stir. Cook on high for 2 1/2 to 3 hours, stirring occasionally.

Chicken & Rice Casserole

1 jar Chicken & Rice
   Casserole Mix

1 - 1 1/2 lbs. chicken breast,
   diced

    Empty contents of jar into slow cooker, stirring to combine. In a saucepan, bring 4 1/2 cups water to a boil. Pour water over rice mixture and stir. In a sauté pan, brown chicken. Add to crock and stir. Cook on high for 2 1/2 to 3 hours, stirring occasionally.

Chicken & Rice Casserole

1 jar Chicken & Rice
   Casserole Mix

1 - 1 1/2 lbs. chicken breast,
   diced

    Empty contents of jar into slow cooker, stirring to combine. In a saucepan, bring 4 1/2 cups water to a boil. Pour water over rice mixture and stir. In a sauté pan, brown chicken. Add to crock and stir. Cook on high for 2 1/2 to 3 hours, stirring occasionally.

Chicken & Rice Casserole

1 jar Chicken & Rice
   Casserole Mix

1 - 1 1/2 lbs. chicken breast,
   diced

    Empty contents of jar into slow cooker, stirring to combine. In a saucepan, bring 4 1/2 cups water to a boil. Pour water over rice mixture and stir. In a sauté pan, brown chicken. Add to crock and stir. Cook on high for 2 1/2 to 3 hours, stirring occasionally.

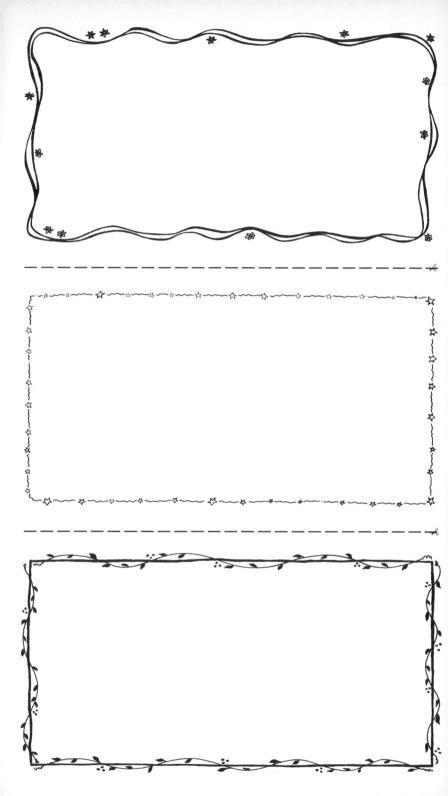

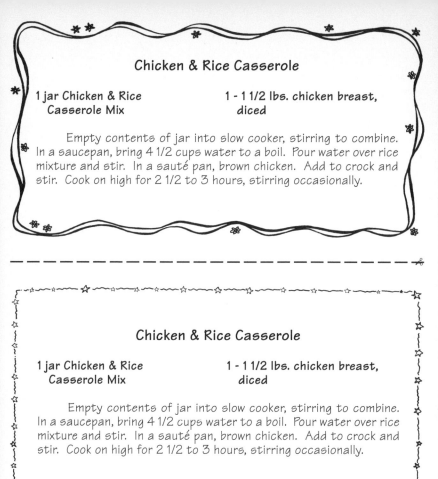

Chicken & Rice Casserole

1 jar Chicken & Rice
Casserole Mix

1 - 1 1/2 lbs. chicken breast,
diced

Empty contents of jar into slow cooker, stirring to combine. In a saucepan, bring 4 1/2 cups water to a boil. Pour water over rice mixture and stir. In a sauté pan, brown chicken. Add to crock and stir. Cook on high for 2 1/2 to 3 hours, stirring occasionally.

Chicken & Rice Casserole

1 jar Chicken & Rice
Casserole Mix

1 - 1 1/2 lbs. chicken breast,
diced

Empty contents of jar into slow cooker, stirring to combine. In a saucepan, bring 4 1/2 cups water to a boil. Pour water over rice mixture and stir. In a sauté pan, brown chicken. Add to crock and stir. Cook on high for 2 1/2 to 3 hours, stirring occasionally.

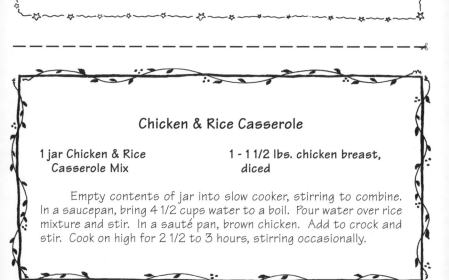

Chicken & Rice Casserole

1 jar Chicken & Rice
Casserole Mix

1 - 1 1/2 lbs. chicken breast,
diced

Empty contents of jar into slow cooker, stirring to combine. In a saucepan, bring 4 1/2 cups water to a boil. Pour water over rice mixture and stir. In a sauté pan, brown chicken. Add to crock and stir. Cook on high for 2 1/2 to 3 hours, stirring occasionally.

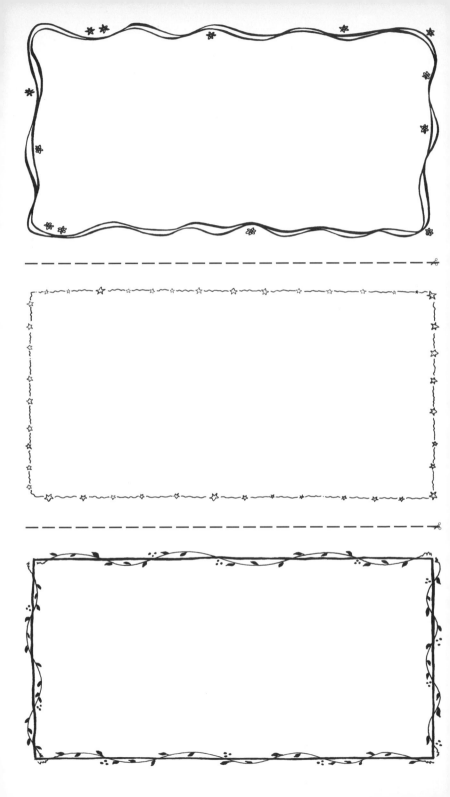

Apple Dumpling Coffee Cake Mix

1 3/4 C. rolled oats
1 C. brown sugar
1 1/2 C. flour
1 1/2 tsp. baking powder
2 tsp. cinnamon
1/2 tsp. nutmeg

Layer the ingredients in the order given into a wide-mouth 1-quart canning jar. Pack each layer into place before adding the next ingredient.

Attach a gift tag with the mixing and cooking instructions.

❋ *Gifts in a Jar make great bake sale items.* ❋

Apple Dumpling Coffee Cake

1 jar Apple Dumpling Coffee
   Cake Mix
1/2 C. butter or margarine
1 egg
1/2 C. whole milk
5 -6 tart apples, cored, peeled
   and sliced
1/3 C. sugar

Empty contents of jar into a large mixing bowl, stirring to combine. Cut butter into dry ingredients. Whisk together egg and milk and stir into butter mixture. Knead a few times by hand or spoon until mixture resembles a wet biscuit dough. Butter bottom and sides of slow cooker. Layer apples over the bottom of crock. Sprinkle sugar over apples and drop spoonfuls of dough over the apples so they are mostly covered. Cook on high for 2 to 2 1/2 hours.

Apple Dumpling Coffee Cake

1 jar Apple Dumpling Coffee
   Cake Mix
1/2 C. butter or margarine
1 egg

1/2 C. whole milk
5 -6 tart apples, cored, peeled
   and sliced
1/3 C. sugar

    Empty contents of jar into a large mixing bowl, stirring to combine. Cut butter into dry ingredients. Whisk together egg and milk and stir into butter mixture. Knead a few times by hand or spoon until mixture resembles a wet biscuit dough. Butter bottom and sides of slow cooker. Layer apples over the bottom of crock. Sprinkle sugar over apples and drop spoonfuls of dough over the apples so they are mostly covered. Cook on high for 2 to 2 1/2 hours.

Apple Dumpling Coffee Cake

1 jar Apple Dumpling Coffee
   Cake Mix
1/2 C. butter or margarine
1 egg

1/2 C. whole milk
5 -6 tart apples, cored, peeled
   and sliced
1/3 C. sugar

    Empty contents of jar into a large mixing bowl, stirring to combine. Cut butter into dry ingredients. Whisk together egg and milk and stir into butter mixture. Knead a few times by hand or spoon until mixture resembles a wet biscuit dough. Butter bottom and sides of slow cooker. Layer apples over the bottom of crock. Sprinkle sugar over apples and drop spoonfuls of dough over the apples so they are mostly covered. Cook on high for 2 to 2 1/2 hours.

Apple Dumpling Coffee Cake

1 jar Apple Dumpling Coffee
   Cake Mix
1/2 C. butter or margarine
1 egg

1/2 C. whole milk
5 -6 tart apples, cored, peeled
   and sliced
1/3 C. sugar

    Empty contents of jar into a large mixing bowl, stirring to combine. Cut butter into dry ingredients. Whisk together egg and milk and stir into butter mixture. Knead a few times by hand or spoon until mixture resembles a wet biscuit dough. Butter bottom and sides of slow cooker. Layer apples over the bottom of crock. Sprinkle sugar over apples and drop spoonfuls of dough over the apples so they are mostly covered. Cook on high for 2 to 2 1/2 hours.

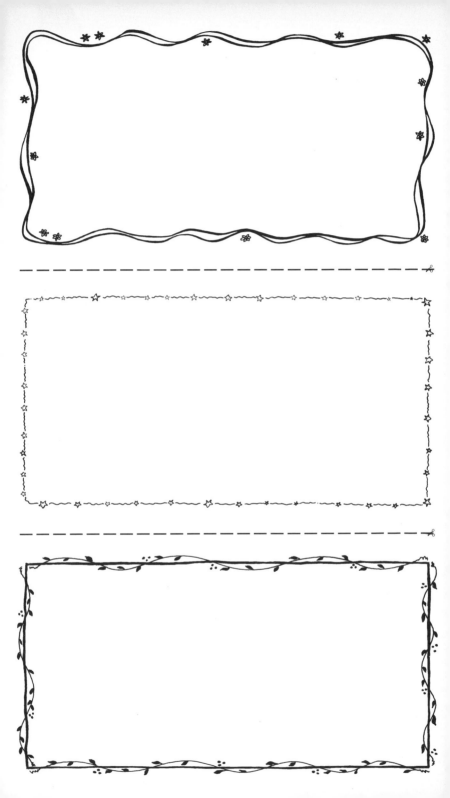

Apple Dumpling Coffee Cake

1 jar Apple Dumpling Coffee
   Cake Mix
1/2 C. butter or margarine
1 egg

1/2 C. whole milk
5 -6 tart apples, cored, peeled
   and sliced
1/3 C. sugar

Empty contents of jar into a large mixing bowl, stirring to combine. Cut butter into dry ingredients. Whisk together egg and milk and stir into butter mixture. Knead a few times by hand or spoon until mixture resembles a wet biscuit dough. Butter bottom and sides of slow cooker. Layer apples over the bottom of crock. Sprinkle sugar over apples and drop spoonfuls of dough over the apples so they are mostly covered. Cook on high for 2 to 2 1/2 hours.

Apple Dumpling Coffee Cake

1 jar Apple Dumpling Coffee
   Cake Mix
1/2 C. butter or margarine
1 egg

1/2 C. whole milk
5 -6 tart apples, cored, peeled
   and sliced
1/3 C. sugar

Empty contents of jar into a large mixing bowl, stirring to combine. Cut butter into dry ingredients. Whisk together egg and milk and stir into butter mixture. Knead a few times by hand or spoon until mixture resembles a wet biscuit dough. Butter bottom and sides of slow cooker. Layer apples over the bottom of crock. Sprinkle sugar over apples and drop spoonfuls of dough over the apples so they are mostly covered. Cook on high for 2 to 2 1/2 hours.

Apple Dumpling Coffee Cake

1 jar Apple Dumpling Coffee
   Cake Mix
1/2 C. butter or margarine
1 egg

1/2 C. whole milk
5 -6 tart apples, cored, peeled
   and sliced
1/3 C. sugar

Empty contents of jar into a large mixing bowl, stirring to combine. Cut butter into dry ingredients. Whisk together egg and milk and stir into butter mixture. Knead a few times by hand or spoon until mixture resembles a wet biscuit dough. Butter bottom and sides of slow cooker. Layer apples over the bottom of crock. Sprinkle sugar over apples and drop spoonfuls of dough over the apples so they are mostly covered. Cook on high for 2 to 2 1/2 hours.

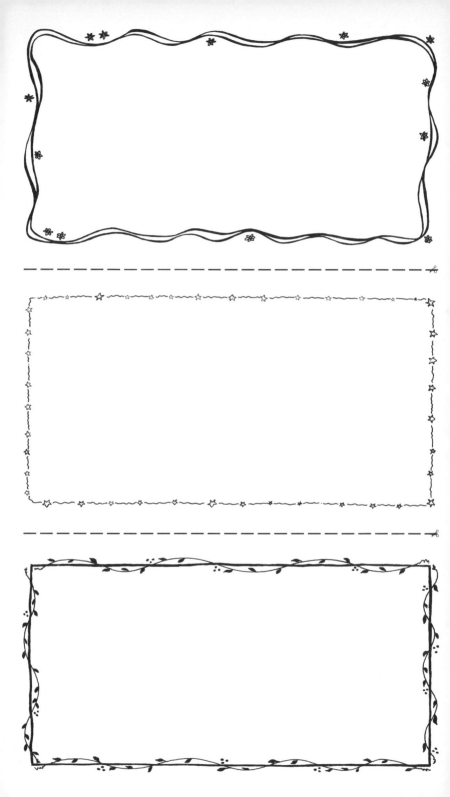

Beef Stroganoff with Noodles Mix

1 pkg. Knorr® White Sauce
1 pkg. Knorr® Classic Brown
   Gravy Mix
1 T. dried dill
1 T. dried parsley
3 2/3 C. medium egg noodles

Layer the ingredients in the order given into a wide-mouth 1-quart canning jar. Pack each layer into place before adding the next ingredient.

Attach a gift tag with the cooking instructions.

Beef Stroganoff with Noodles

1 jar Beef Stroganoff with
  Noodles Mix
2 C. whole milk
1 - 2 lbs. cubed beef

Empty contents of jar into slow cooker, stirring to combine. In a saucepan, bring 2 cups water and milk to a simmer. Pour over dry ingredients, stirring with a whisk to fully incorporate sauce. In a sauté pan, brown beef then add to crock. Cook on high for 3 hours.

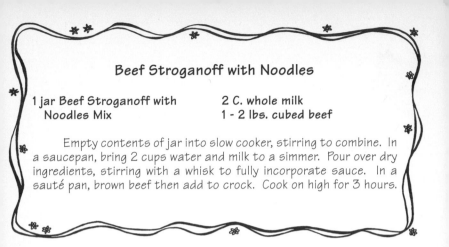

Beef Stroganoff with Noodles

1 jar Beef Stroganoff with
    Noodles Mix

2 C. whole milk
1 - 2 lbs. cubed beef

Empty contents of jar into slow cooker, stirring to combine. In a saucepan, bring 2 cups water and milk to a simmer. Pour over dry ingredients, stirring with a whisk to fully incorporate sauce. In a sauté pan, brown beef then add to crock. Cook on high for 3 hours.

Beef Stroganoff with Noodles

1 jar Beef Stroganoff with
    Noodles Mix

2 C. whole milk
1 - 2 lbs. cubed beef

Empty contents of jar into slow cooker, stirring to combine. In a saucepan, bring 2 cups water and milk to a simmer. Pour over dry ingredients, stirring with a whisk to fully incorporate sauce. In a sauté pan, brown beef then add to crock. Cook on high for 3 hours.

Beef Stroganoff with Noodles

1 jar Beef Stroganoff with
    Noodles Mix

2 C. whole milk
1 - 2 lbs. cubed beef

Empty contents of jar into slow cooker, stirring to combine. In a saucepan, bring 2 cups water and milk to a simmer. Pour over dry ingredients, stirring with a whisk to fully incorporate sauce. In a sauté pan, brown beef then add to crock. Cook on high for 3 hours.

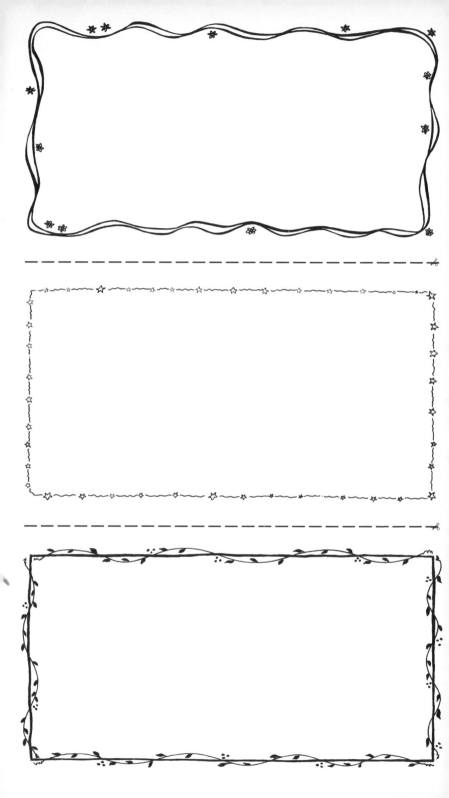

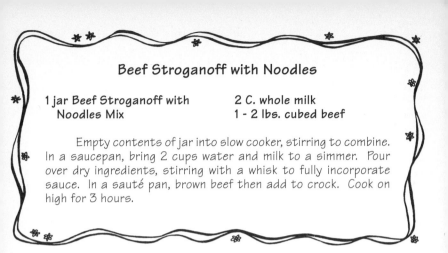

Beef Stroganoff with Noodles

1 jar Beef Stroganoff with
    Noodles Mix

2 C. whole milk
1 - 2 lbs. cubed beef

Empty contents of jar into slow cooker, stirring to combine. In a saucepan, bring 2 cups water and milk to a simmer. Pour over dry ingredients, stirring with a whisk to fully incorporate sauce. In a sauté pan, brown beef then add to crock. Cook on high for 3 hours.

Beef Stroganoff with Noodles

1 jar Beef Stroganoff with
    Noodles Mix

2 C. whole milk
1 - 2 lbs. cubed beef

Empty contents of jar into slow cooker, stirring to combine. In a saucepan, bring 2 cups water and milk to a simmer. Pour over dry ingredients, stirring with a whisk to fully incorporate sauce. In a sauté pan, brown beef then add to crock. Cook on high for 3 hours.

Beef Stroganoff with Noodles

1 jar Beef Stroganoff with
    Noodles Mix

2 C. whole milk
1 - 2 lbs. cubed beef

Empty contents of jar into slow cooker, stirring to combine. In a saucepan, bring 2 cups water and milk to a simmer. Pour over dry ingredients, stirring with a whisk to fully incorporate sauce. In a sauté pan, brown beef then add to crock. Cook on high for 3 hours.

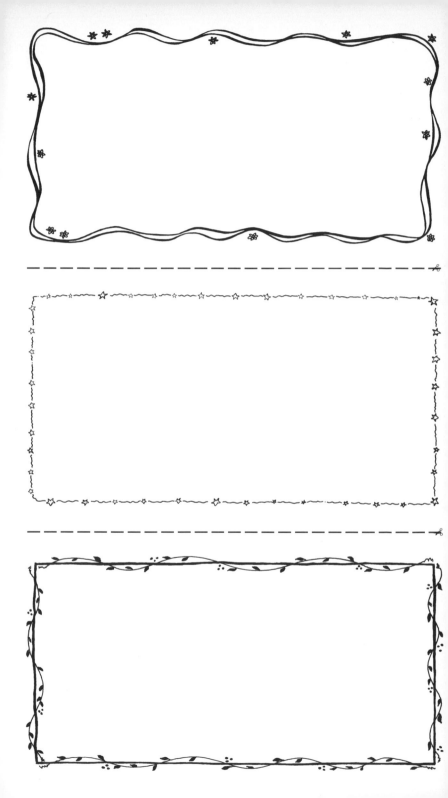

Meat & Potato Pie Mix

1 T. dried parsley
1 tsp. salt
3 C. instant mashed potatoes

Seasoning Packet:
1 C. fine bread crumbs
1 T. dried minced onion
1 tsp. dried thyme
2 tsp. salt
1 tsp. pepper
1 T. dried celery flakes

Layer the ingredients in the order given into a wide-mouth 1-quart canning jar. Mix and place the seasonings in a small plastic bag. Place the packet on top of the potatoes.

Attach a gift tag with the cooking instructions.

Meat & Potato Pie

1 jar Meat & Potato Pie Mix
2 eggs
1 C. milk
3 lbs. lean ground beef or pork
1/4 C. butter
1 1/2 C. milk
1 C. shredded Cheddar cheese

In a large bowl, combine eggs, milk and seasoning packet. Let mixture sit for a few minutes to allow bread crumbs to absorb moisture. Knead in beef or pork to make a meat loaf mixture. Put meat into a greased slow cooker, spreading evenly. Cook on high for 2 1/2 hours. Use a basting needle to drain any excess fat. In a saucepan, bring 3 cups water, butter and milk to a boil. Stir in potatoes. Spread over meat layer and top with shredded Cheddar cheese. Cook for 1 hour longer.

Meat & Potato Pie

1 jar Meat & Potato Pie Mix
2 eggs
1 C. milk
3 lbs. lean ground beef or pork

1/4 C. butter
1 1/2 C. milk
1 C. shredded Cheddar cheese

In a large bowl, combine eggs, milk and seasoning packet. Let mixture sit for a few minutes to allow bread crumbs to absorb moisture. Knead in beef or pork to make a meat loaf mixture. Put meat into a greased slow cooker, spreading evenly. Cook on high for 2 1/2 hours. Use a basting needle to drain any excess fat. In a saucepan, bring 3 cups water, butter and milk to a boil. Stir in potatoes. Spread over meat layer and top with shredded Cheddar cheese. Cook for 1 hour longer.

Meat & Potato Pie

1 jar Meat & Potato Pie Mix
2 eggs
1 C. milk
3 lbs. lean ground beef or pork

1/4 C. butter
1 1/2 C. milk
1 C. shredded Cheddar cheese

In a large bowl, combine eggs, milk and seasoning packet. Let mixture sit for a few minutes to allow bread crumbs to absorb moisture. Knead in beef or pork to make a meat loaf mixture. Put meat into a greased slow cooker, spreading evenly. Cook on high for 2 1/2 hours. Use a basting needle to drain any excess fat. In a saucepan, bring 3 cups water, butter and milk to a boil. Stir in potatoes. Spread over meat layer and top with shredded Cheddar cheese. Cook for 1 hour longer.

Meat & Potato Pie

1 jar Meat & Potato Pie Mix
2 eggs
1 C. milk
3 lbs. lean ground beef or pork

1/4 C. butter
1 1/2 C. milk
1 C. shredded Cheddar cheese

In a large bowl, combine eggs, milk and seasoning packet. Let mixture sit for a few minutes to allow bread crumbs to absorb moisture. Knead in beef or pork to make a meat loaf mixture. Put meat into a greased slow cooker, spreading evenly. Cook on high for 2 1/2 hours. Use a basting needle to drain any excess fat. In a saucepan, bring 3 cups water, butter and milk to a boil. Stir in potatoes. Spread over meat layer and top with shredded Cheddar cheese. Cook for 1 hour longer.

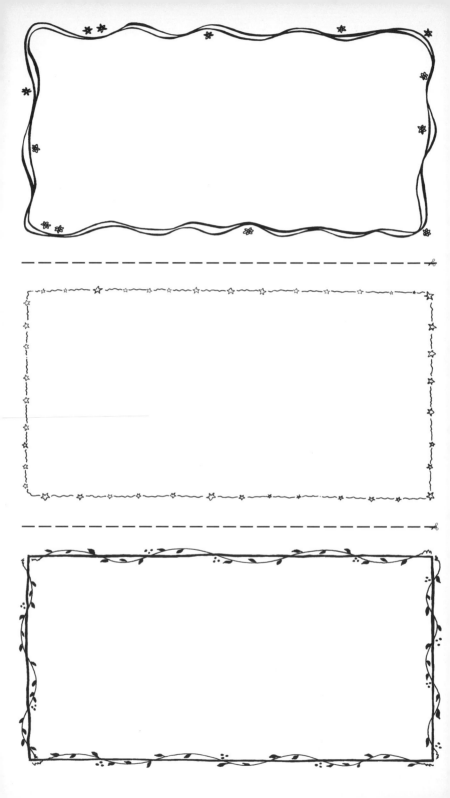

Meat & Potato Pie

1 jar Meat & Potato Pie Mix   1/4 C. butter
2 eggs   1 1/2 C. milk
1 C. milk   1 C. shredded Cheddar cheese
3 lbs. lean ground beef or pork

In a large bowl, combine eggs, milk and seasoning packet. Let mixture sit for a few minutes to allow bread crumbs to absorb moisture. Knead in beef or pork to make a meat loaf mixture. Put meat into a greased slow cooker, spreading evenly. Cook on high for 2 1/2 hours. Use a basting needle to drain any excess fat. In a saucepan, bring 3 cups water, butter and milk to a boil. Stir in potatoes. Spread over meat layer and top with shredded Cheddar cheese. Cook for 1 hour longer.

Meat & Potato Pie

1 jar Meat & Potato Pie Mix   1/4 C. butter
2 eggs   1 1/2 C. milk
1 C. milk   1 C. shredded Cheddar cheese
3 lbs. lean ground beef or pork

In a large bowl, combine eggs, milk and seasoning packet. Let mixture sit for a few minutes to allow bread crumbs to absorb moisture. Knead in beef or pork to make a meat loaf mixture. Put meat into a greased slow cooker, spreading evenly. Cook on high for 2 1/2 hours. Use a basting needle to drain any excess fat. In a saucepan, bring 3 cups water, butter and milk to a boil. Stir in potatoes. Spread over meat layer and top with shredded Cheddar cheese. Cook for 1 hour longer.

Meat & Potato Pie

1 jar Meat & Potato Pie Mix   1/4 C. butter
2 eggs   1 1/2 C. milk
1 C. milk   1 C. shredded Cheddar cheese
3 lbs. lean ground beef or pork

In a large bowl, combine eggs, milk and seasoning packet. Let mixture sit for a few minutes to allow bread crumbs to absorb moisture. Knead in beef or pork to make a meat loaf mixture. Put meat into a greased slow cooker, spreading evenly. Cook on high for 2 1/2 hours. Use a basting needle to drain any excess fat. In a saucepan, bring 3 cups water, butter and milk to a boil. Stir in potatoes. Spread over meat layer and top with shredded Cheddar cheese. Cook for 1 hour longer.

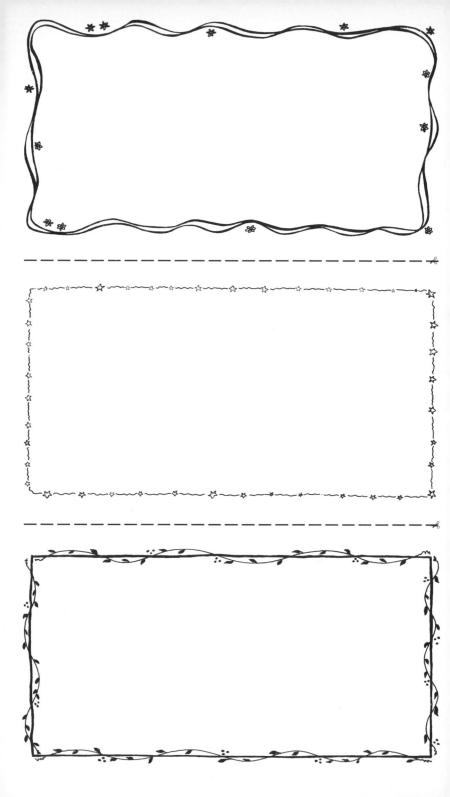

Christmas Bread Pudding Mix

1 tsp. cinnamon
1/2 C. sugar
1/4 C. dried tart cherries
1/4 C. golden raisins
1/4 C. currants
3 C. store-bought unseasoned
  dried bread cubes

Layer the ingredients in the order given into a wide-mouth 1-quart canning jar. Pack each layer into place before adding the next ingredient.

Attach a gift tag with the mixing and cooking instructions.

❀ At times, it may seem impossible to make all of the jar ingredients fit, but with persistence, they do all fit. ❀

Christmas Bread Pudding

1 jar Christmas Bread
   Pudding Mix
1 Qt. whole milk
2 eggs
1 tsp. vanilla

Grease bottom and sides of slow cooker. Empty contents of jar into the crock, stirring to combine. In a saucepan, bring milk to a simmer then pour over bread mixture. Let rest for 10 minutes allowing milk to cool and bread to absorb liquid. Whisk together eggs and vanilla and stir into bread mixture until fully incorporated. Cook on high for 1 1/2 to 2 hours.

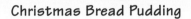

Christmas Bread Pudding

1 jar Christmas Bread
   Pudding Mix
1 Qt. whole milk

2 eggs
1 tsp. vanilla

Grease bottom and sides of slow cooker. Empty contents of jar into the crock, stirring to combine. In a saucepan, bring milk to a simmer then pour over bread mixture. Let rest for 10 minutes allowing milk to cool and bread to absorb liquid. Whisk together eggs and vanilla and stir into bread mixture until fully incorporated. Cook on high for 1 1/2 to 2 hours.

Christmas Bread Pudding

1 jar Christmas Bread
   Pudding Mix
1 Qt. whole milk

2 eggs
1 tsp. vanilla

Grease bottom and sides of slow cooker. Empty contents of jar into the crock, stirring to combine. In a saucepan, bring milk to a simmer then pour over bread mixture. Let rest for 10 minutes allowing milk to cool and bread to absorb liquid. Whisk together eggs and vanilla and stir into bread mixture until fully incorporated. Cook on high for 1 1/2 to 2 hours.

Christmas Bread Pudding

1 jar Christmas Bread
   Pudding Mix
1 Qt. whole milk

2 eggs
1 tsp. vanilla

Grease bottom and sides of slow cooker. Empty contents of jar into the crock, stirring to combine. In a saucepan, bring milk to a simmer then pour over bread mixture. Let rest for 10 minutes allowing milk to cool and bread to absorb liquid. Whisk together eggs and vanilla and stir into bread mixture until fully incorporated. Cook on high for 1 1/2 to 2 hours.

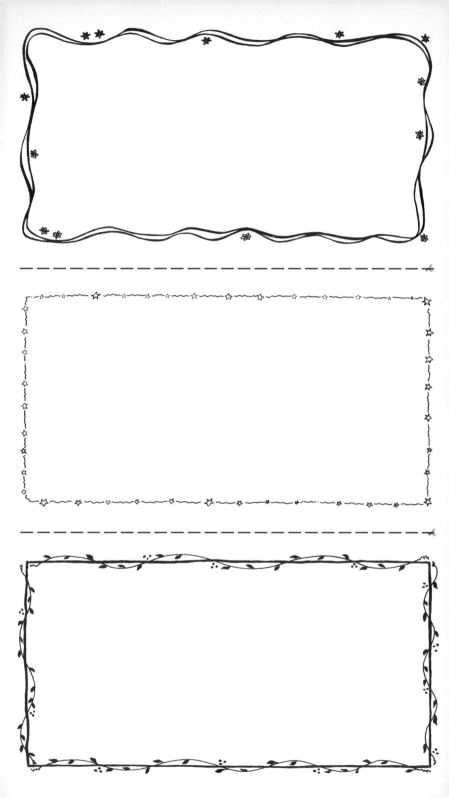

Christmas Bread Pudding

1 jar Christmas Bread
   Pudding Mix
1 Qt. whole milk

2 eggs
1 tsp. vanilla

    Grease bottom and sides of slow cooker. Empty contents of jar into the crock, stirring to combine. In a saucepan, bring milk to a simmer then pour over bread mixture. Let rest for 10 minutes allowing milk to cool and bread to absorb liquid. Whisk together eggs and vanilla and stir into bread mixture until fully incorporated. Cook on high for 1 1/2 to 2 hours.

Christmas Bread Pudding

1 jar Christmas Bread
   Pudding Mix
1 Qt. whole milk

2 eggs
1 tsp. vanilla

    Grease bottom and sides of slow cooker. Empty contents of jar into the crock, stirring to combine. In a saucepan, bring milk to a simmer then pour over bread mixture. Let rest for 10 minutes allowing milk to cool and bread to absorb liquid. Whisk together eggs and vanilla and stir into bread mixture until fully incorporated. Cook on high for 1 1/2 to 2 hours.

Christmas Bread Pudding

1 jar Christmas Bread
   Pudding Mix
1 Qt. whole milk

2 eggs
1 tsp. vanilla

    Grease bottom and sides of slow cooker. Empty contents of jar into the crock, stirring to combine. In a saucepan, bring milk to a simmer then pour over bread mixture. Let rest for 10 minutes allowing milk to cool and bread to absorb liquid. Whisk together eggs and vanilla and stir into bread mixture until fully incorporated. Cook on high for 1 1/2 to 2 hours.

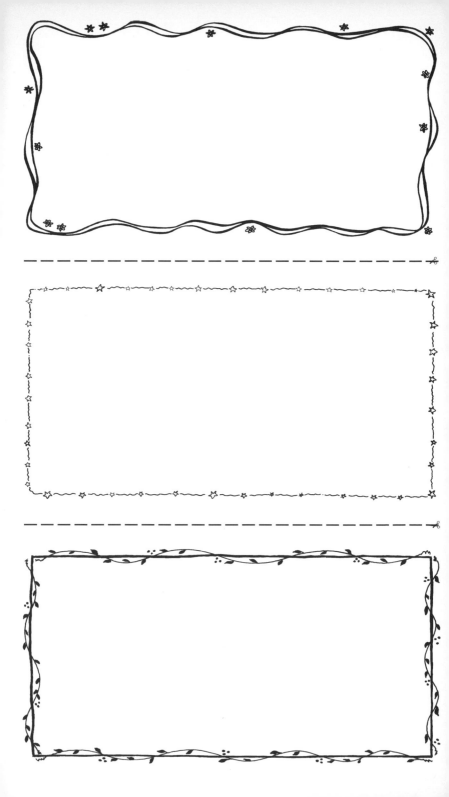

Italian Tortellini Soup Mix

1 1/2 T. chicken bouillon
1 T. dried basil
1 T. dried parsley
1 1/2 tsp. oregano
2 tsp. dried minced garlic
2 1/2 C. dried tortellini pasta

1 1/2 C. red kidney beans in
   a baggie

Layer the ingredients in the order given into a wide-mouth 1-quart canning jar. Place beans on top of the pasta.

Attach a gift tag with the cooking instructions.

Italian Tortellini Soup

1 jar Italian Tortellini Soup Mix
1 (29 oz.) can diced tomatoes
with juice

Remove beans from Italian Tortellini Soup Mix. Wash beans then place in a microwave safe dish, filling with water 1 to 1 1/2 inches over the beans. Cover tightly with plastic wrap, poking three small holes in the top with a sharp knife. Microwave on high for 9 minutes, rotate and microwave for another 9 minutes. Drain beans, and place in slow cooker. Cover with 6 to 8 cups hot water. Cook on high for 2 hours. Add remaining jar ingredients and tomatoes. Cook on high for another 1 to 1 1/2 hours.

Italian Tortellini Soup

1 jar Italian Tortellini Soup
 Mix

1 (29 oz.) can diced tomatoes
 with juice

Remove beans from Italian Tortellini Soup Mix. Wash beans then place in a microwave safe dish, filling with water 1 to 1 1/2 inches over the beans. Cover tightly with plastic wrap, poking three small holes in the top with a sharp knife. Microwave on high for 9 minutes, rotate and microwave for another 9 minutes. Drain beans, and place in slow cooker. Cover with 6 to 8 cups hot water. Cook on high for 2 hours. Add remaining jar ingredients and tomatoes. Cook on high for another 1 to 1 1/2 hours.

Italian Tortellini Soup

1 jar Italian Tortellini Soup
 Mix

1 (29 oz.) can diced tomatoes
 with juice

Remove beans from Italian Tortellini Soup Mix. Wash beans then place in a microwave safe dish, filling with water 1 to 1 1/2 inches over the beans. Cover tightly with plastic wrap, poking three small holes in the top with a sharp knife. Microwave on high for 9 minutes, rotate and microwave for another 9 minutes. Drain beans, and place in slow cooker. Cover with 6 to 8 cups hot water. Cook on high for 2 hours. Add remaining jar ingredients and tomatoes. Cook on high for another 1 to 1 1/2 hours.

Italian Tortellini Soup

1 jar Italian Tortellini Soup
 Mix

1 (29 oz.) can diced tomatoes
 with juice

Remove beans from Italian Tortellini Soup Mix. Wash beans then place in a microwave safe dish, filling with water 1 to 1 1/2 inches over the beans. Cover tightly with plastic wrap, poking three small holes in the top with a sharp knife. Microwave on high for 9 minutes, rotate and microwave for another 9 minutes. Drain beans, and place in slow cooker. Cover with 6 to 8 cups hot water. Cook on high for 2 hours. Add remaining jar ingredients and tomatoes. Cook on high for another 1 to 1 1/2 hours.

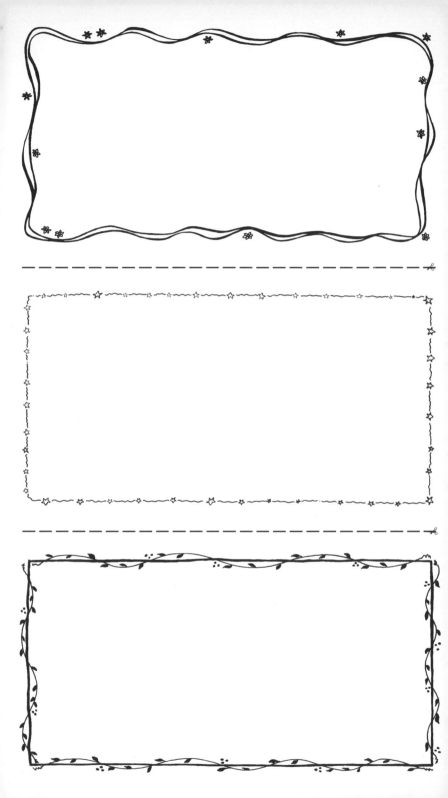

Italian Tortellini Soup

1 jar Italian Tortellini Soup
   Mix

1 (29 oz.) can diced tomatoes
   with juice

Remove beans from Italian Tortellini Soup Mix. Wash beans then place in a microwave safe dish, filling with water 1 to 1 1/2 inches over the beans. Cover tightly with plastic wrap, poking three small holes in the top with a sharp knife. Microwave on high for 9 minutes, rotate and microwave for another 9 minutes. Drain beans, and place in slow cooker. Cover with 6 to 8 cups hot water. Cook on high for 2 hours. Add remaining jar ingredients and tomatoes. Cook on high for another 1 to 1 1/2 hours.

Italian Tortellini Soup

1 jar Italian Tortellini Soup
   Mix

1 (29 oz.) can diced tomatoes
   with juice

Remove beans from Italian Tortellini Soup Mix. Wash beans then place in a microwave safe dish, filling with water 1 to 1 1/2 inches over the beans. Cover tightly with plastic wrap, poking three small holes in the top with a sharp knife. Microwave on high for 9 minutes, rotate and microwave for another 9 minutes. Drain beans, and place in slow cooker. Cover with 6 to 8 cups hot water. Cook on high for 2 hours. Add remaining jar ingredients and tomatoes. Cook on high for another 1 to 1 1/2 hours.

Italian Tortellini Soup

1 jar Italian Tortellini Soup
   Mix

1 (29 oz.) can diced tomatoes
   with juice

Remove beans from Italian Tortellini Soup Mix. Wash beans then place in a microwave safe dish, filling with water 1 to 1 1/2 inches over the beans. Cover tightly with plastic wrap, poking three small holes in the top with a sharp knife. Microwave on high for 9 minutes, rotate and microwave for another 9 minutes. Drain beans, and place in slow cooker. Cover with 6 to 8 cups hot water. Cook on high for 2 hours. Add remaining jar ingredients and tomatoes. Cook on high for another 1 to 1 1/2 hours.

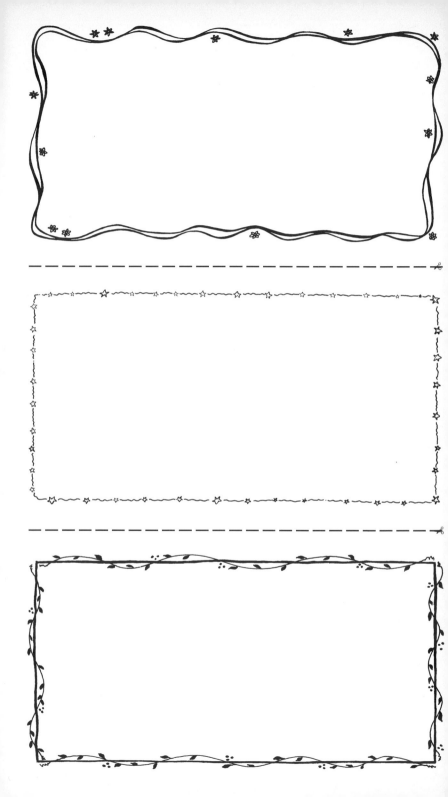

Old Fashioned Macaroni & Cheese Mix

1 pkg. Knorr® White Sauce
1/3 C. Parmesan cheese
1/4 C. real bacon bits
1 T. dried minced onion
1 T. dried parsley
3 1/2 C. elbow macaroni

Layer the ingredients in the order given into a wide-mouth 1-quart canning jar. Pack each layer into place before adding the next ingredient.

Attach a gift tag with the cooking instructions.

Old Fashioned Macaroni & Cheese

1 jar Old Fashioned Macaroni
   & Cheese Mix
5 C. whole milk
3/4 C. shredded sharp
   Cheddar cheese

Empty contents of jar into slow cooker, stirring to combine. In a saucepan, bring milk to a boil and pour over dry ingredients, stirring with a whisk to fully incorporate sauce. Cook on high for 2 to 3 hours. Add cheese to macaroni and stir in or leave as a cheesy top layer. Cook on high for another 1/2 hour.

Old Fashioned Macaroni & Cheese

1 jar Old Fashioned Macaroni
   & Cheese Mix
5 C. whole milk

3/4 C. shredded sharp Cheddar
   cheese

Empty contents of jar into slow cooker, stirring to combine. In a saucepan, bring milk to a boil and pour over dry ingredients, stirring with a whisk to fully incorporate sauce. Cook on high for 2 to 3 hours. Add cheese to macaroni and stir in or leave as a cheesy top layer. Cook on high for another 1/2 hour.

Old Fashioned Macaroni & Cheese

1 jar Old Fashioned Macaroni
   & Cheese Mix
5 C. whole milk

3/4 C. shredded sharp Cheddar
   cheese

Empty contents of jar into slow cooker, stirring to combine. In a saucepan, bring milk to a boil and pour over dry ingredients, stirring with a whisk to fully incorporate sauce. Cook on high for 2 to 3 hours. Add cheese to macaroni and stir in or leave as a cheesy top layer. Cook on high for another 1/2 hour.

Old Fashioned Macaroni & Cheese

1 jar Old Fashioned Macaroni
   & Cheese Mix
5 C. whole milk

3/4 C. shredded sharp Cheddar
   cheese

Empty contents of jar into slow cooker, stirring to combine. In a saucepan, bring milk to a boil and pour over dry ingredients, stirring with a whisk to fully incorporate sauce. Cook on high for 2 to 3 hours. Add cheese to macaroni and stir in or leave as a cheesy top layer. Cook on high for another 1/2 hour.

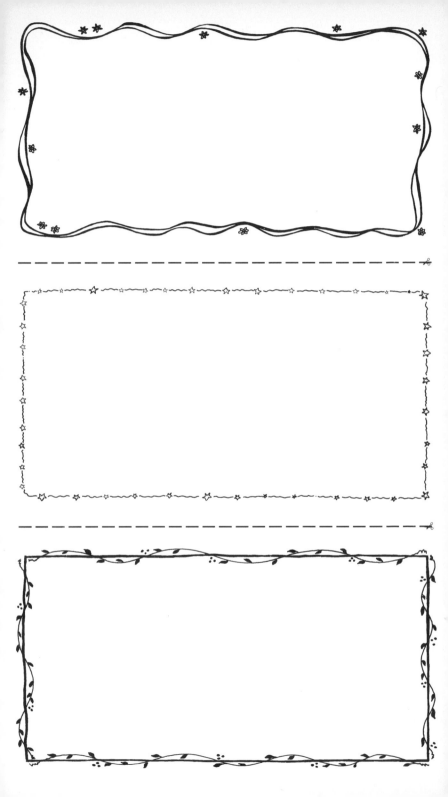

Old Fashioned Macaroni & Cheese

1 jar Old Fashioned Macaroni   3/4 C. shredded sharp Cheddar
   & Cheese Mix   cheese
5 C. whole milk

    Empty contents of jar into slow cooker, stirring to combine. In a saucepan, bring milk to a boil and pour over dry ingredients, stirring with a whisk to fully incorporate sauce. Cook on high for 2 to 3 hours. Add cheese to macaroni and stir in or leave as a cheesy top layer. Cook on high for another 1/2 hour.

Old Fashioned Macaroni & Cheese

1 jar Old Fashioned Macaroni   3/4 C. shredded sharp Cheddar
   & Cheese Mix   cheese
5 C. whole milk

    Empty contents of jar into slow cooker, stirring to combine. In a saucepan, bring milk to a boil and pour over dry ingredients, stirring with a whisk to fully incorporate sauce. Cook on high for 2 to 3 hours. Add cheese to macaroni and stir in or leave as a cheesy top layer. Cook on high for another 1/2 hour.

Old Fashioned Macaroni & Cheese

1 jar Old Fashioned Macaroni   3/4 C. shredded sharp Cheddar
   & Cheese Mix   cheese
5 C. whole milk

    Empty contents of jar into slow cooker, stirring to combine. In a saucepan, bring milk to a boil and pour over dry ingredients, stirring with a whisk to fully incorporate sauce. Cook on high for 2 to 3 hours. Add cheese to macaroni and stir in or leave as a cheesy top layer. Cook on high for another 1/2 hour.

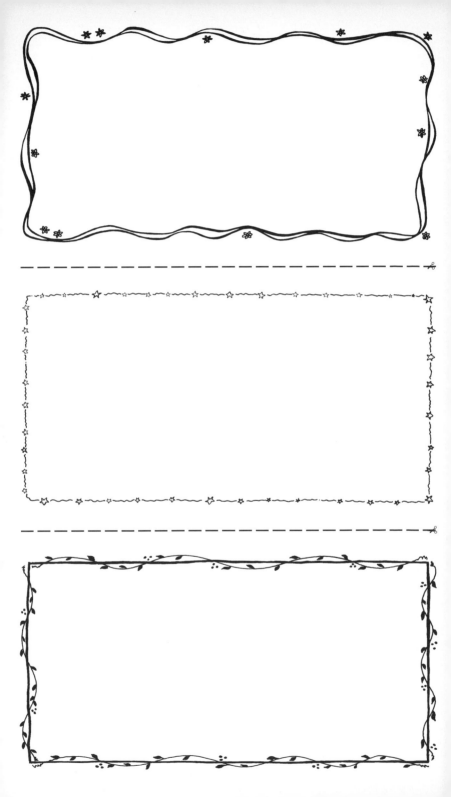

Caramel Rum Fondue Mix

1/2 C. brown sugar
1/2 C. white sugar
40 pieces (10 - 12 oz.) caramel
   candies, unwrapped
2 C. mini marshmallows

Layer the ingredients in the order given into a wide-mouth 1-quart canning jar. Pack each layer into place before adding the next ingredient.

Attach a gift tag with the cooking instructions.

❁ *For an out of the ordinary gift, try placing the mix in a mixing bowl along with kitchen utensils, cookbooks, recipe cards, towels, potholders, and cookie cutters.* ❁

Caramel Rum Fondue

1 jar Caramel Rum Fondue Mix
3/4 C. whipping cream or
    whole milk
1 T. rum or 1/2 tsp. rum flavoring

Empty contents of jar into slow cooker, stirring to mix. Turn slow cooker on high heat. Add whipping cream or milk. Be sure to stir every ten minutes. Once caramels are melted, add rum or rum flavoring. Continue stirring every ten minutes. Makes a great dessert fondue for fruits and pound cake.

Caramel Rum Fondue

1 jar Caramel Rum Fondue Mix	1 T. rum or 1/2 tsp. rum
3/4 C. whipping cream or	flavoring
whole milk	

Empty contents of jar into slow cooker, stirring to mix. Turn slow cooker on high heat. Add whipping cream or milk. Be sure to stir every ten minutes. Once caramels are melted, add rum or rum flavoring. Continue stirring every ten minutes. Makes a great dessert fondue for fruits and pound cake.

Caramel Rum Fondue

1 jar Caramel Rum Fondue Mix   1 T. rum or 1/2 tsp. rum
3/4 C. whipping cream or   flavoring
  whole milk

Empty contents of jar into slow cooker, stirring to mix. Turn slow cooker on high heat. Add whipping cream or milk. Be sure to stir every ten minutes. Once caramels are melted, add rum or rum flavoring. Continue stirring every ten minutes. Makes a great dessert fondue for fruits and pound cake.

Caramel Rum Fondue

1 jar Caramel Rum Fondue Mix   1 T. rum or 1/2 tsp. rum
3/4 C. whipping cream or   flavoring
  whole milk

Empty contents of jar into slow cooker, stirring to mix. Turn slow cooker on high heat. Add whipping cream or milk. Be sure to stir every ten minutes. Once caramels are melted, add rum or rum flavoring. Continue stirring every ten minutes. Makes a great dessert fondue for fruits and pound cake.

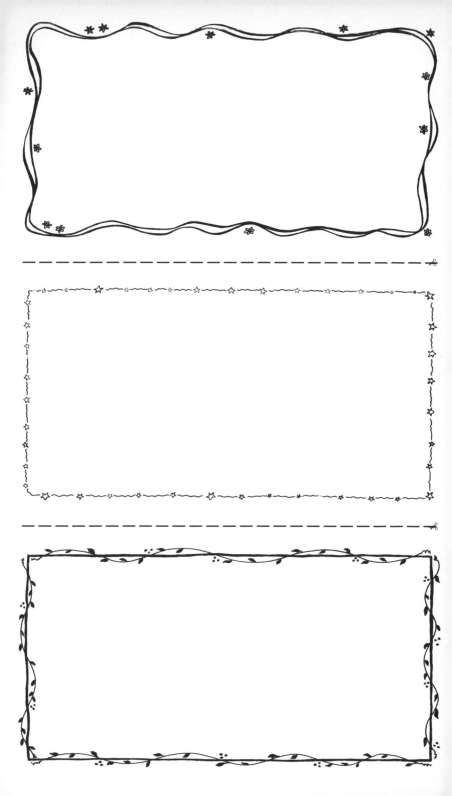

Caramel Rum Fondue

1 jar Caramel Rum Fondue Mix
3/4 C. whipping cream or
  whole milk

1 T. rum or 1/2 tsp. rum
  flavoring

Empty contents of jar into slow cooker, stirring to mix. Turn slow cooker on high heat. Add whipping cream or milk. Be sure to stir every ten minutes. Once caramels are melted, add rum or rum flavoring. Continue stirring every ten minutes. Makes a great dessert fondue for fruits and pound cake.

Caramel Rum Fondue

1 jar Caramel Rum Fondue Mix
3/4 C. whipping cream or
  whole milk

1 T. rum or 1/2 tsp. rum
  flavoring

Empty contents of jar into slow cooker, stirring to mix. Turn slow cooker on high heat. Add whipping cream or milk. Be sure to stir every ten minutes. Once caramels are melted, add rum or rum flavoring. Continue stirring every ten minutes. Makes a great dessert fondue for fruits and pound cake.

Caramel Rum Fondue

1 jar Caramel Rum Fondue Mix
3/4 C. whipping cream or
  whole milk

1 T. rum or 1/2 tsp. rum
  flavoring

Empty contents of jar into slow cooker, stirring to mix. Turn slow cooker on high heat. Add whipping cream or milk. Be sure to stir every ten minutes. Once caramels are melted, add rum or rum flavoring. Continue stirring every ten minutes. Makes a great dessert fondue for fruits and pound cake.

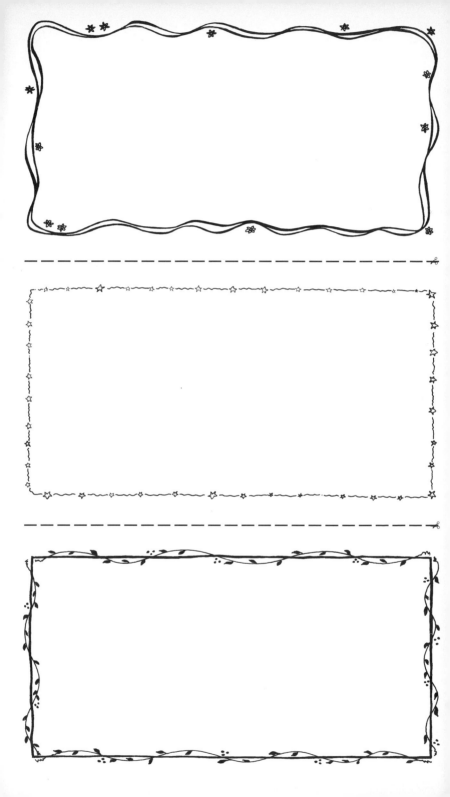

Old Fashioned Brown Bread Mix

1 C. yellow cornmeal
1 C. chopped raisins
1/4 C. brown sugar
1 C. whole wheat flour
1 C. rye flour
2 tsp. baking soda

Layer the ingredients in the order given into a wide-mouth 1-quart canning jar. Pack each layer into place before adding the next ingredient.

Attach a gift tag with the mixing and baking instructions.

❀ Small appliques or embroidery can be added to the center of a fabric cover to further personalize the gift. ❀

Old Fashioned Brown Bread

1 jar Old Fashioned Brown
   Bread Mix
2 C. buttermilk
3/4 C. light or dark molasses

In a large mixing bowl, whisk together buttermilk and molasses. Add contents of jar and stir until well blended. Place greased bread pan or greased tin cans (any heat proof mold that will fit) into slow cooker, filling containers 2/3 full. Cover each mold with greased aluminum foil. Pour boiling water into the slow cooker until it reaches halfway up the sides of the mold. Cook on high for 2 to 3 hours. Allow to cool at least 20 minutes before removing from molds and serving.

Old Fashioned Brown Bread

1 jar Old Fashioned Brown
   Bread Mix

2 C. buttermilk
3/4 C. light or dark molasses

In a large mixing bowl, whisk together buttermilk and molasses. Add contents of jar and stir until well blended. Place greased bread pan or greased tin cans (any heat proof mold that will fit) into slow cooker, filling containers 2/3 full. Cover each mold with greased aluminum foil. Pour boiling water into the slow cooker until it reaches halfway up the sides of the mold. Cook on high for 2 to 3 hours. Allow to cool at least 20 minutes before removing from molds and serving.

Old Fashioned Brown Bread

1 jar Old Fashioned Brown
   Bread Mix

2 C. buttermilk
3/4 C. light or dark molasses

In a large mixing bowl, whisk together buttermilk and molasses. Add contents of jar and stir until well blended. Place greased bread pan or greased tin cans (any heat proof mold that will fit) into slow cooker, filling containers 2/3 full. Cover each mold with greased aluminum foil. Pour boiling water into the slow cooker until it reaches halfway up the sides of the mold. Cook on high for 2 to 3 hours. Allow to cool at least 20 minutes before removing from molds and serving.

Old Fashioned Brown Bread

1 jar Old Fashioned Brown
   Bread Mix

2 C. buttermilk
3/4 C. light or dark molasses

In a large mixing bowl, whisk together buttermilk and molasses. Add contents of jar and stir until well blended. Place greased bread pan or greased tin cans (any heat proof mold that will fit) into slow cooker, filling containers 2/3 full. Cover each mold with greased aluminum foil. Pour boiling water into the slow cooker until it reaches halfway up the sides of the mold. Cook on high for 2 to 3 hours. Allow to cool at least 20 minutes before removing from molds and serving.

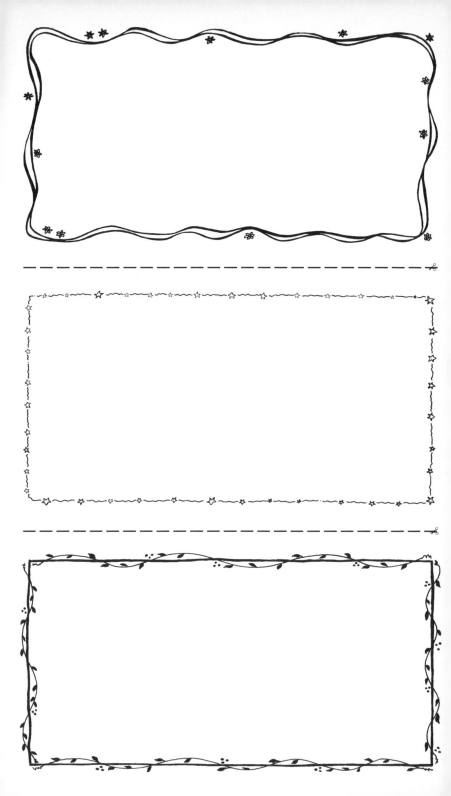

Old Fashioned Brown Bread

1 jar Old Fashioned Brown
  Bread Mix

2 C. buttermilk
3/4 C. light or dark molasses

In a large mixing bowl, whisk together buttermilk and molasses. Add contents of jar and stir until well blended. Place greased bread pan or greased tin cans (any heat proof mold that will fit) into slow cooker, filling containers 2/3 full. Cover each mold with greased aluminum foil. Pour boiling water into the slow cooker until it reaches halfway up the sides of the mold. Cook on high for 2 to 3 hours. Allow to cool at least 20 minutes before removing from molds and serving.

Old Fashioned Brown Bread

1 jar Old Fashioned Brown
  Bread Mix

2 C. buttermilk
3/4 C. light or dark molasses

In a large mixing bowl, whisk together buttermilk and molasses. Add contents of jar and stir until well blended. Place greased bread pan or greased tin cans (any heat proof mold that will fit) into slow cooker, filling containers 2/3 full. Cover each mold with greased aluminum foil. Pour boiling water into the slow cooker until it reaches halfway up the sides of the mold. Cook on high for 2 to 3 hours. Allow to cool at least 20 minutes before removing from molds and serving.

Old Fashioned Brown Bread

1 jar Old Fashioned Brown
  Bread Mix

2 C. buttermilk
3/4 C. light or dark molasses

In a large mixing bowl, whisk together buttermilk and molasses. Add contents of jar and stir until well blended. Place greased bread pan or greased tin cans (any heat proof mold that will fit) into slow cooker, filling containers 2/3 full. Cover each mold with greased aluminum foil. Pour boiling water into the slow cooker until it reaches halfway up the sides of the mold. Cook on high for 2 to 3 hours. Allow to cool at least 20 minutes before removing from molds and serving.

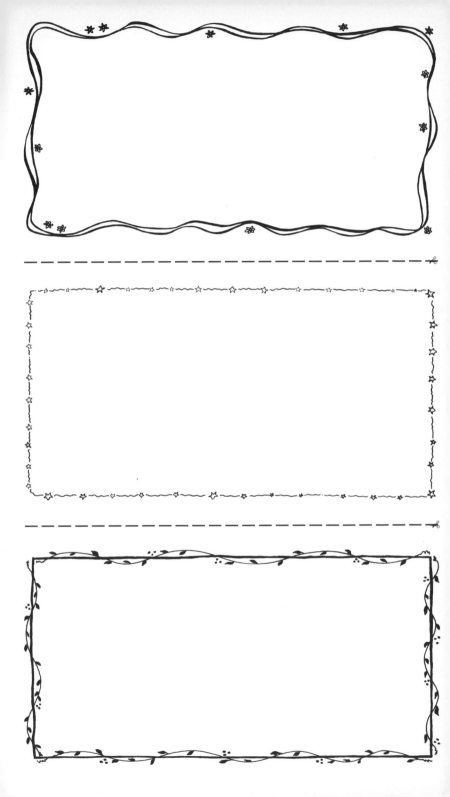

English Beef Pot Pie Mix

2 1/2 C. flour
1 1/2 tsp. baking powder
1 tsp. salt

Seasoning Packet:
1/4 C. dried celery flakes
1/4 C. beef bouillon
2 T. dried minced onion
1 T. dried parsley
1/2 C. flour
1 tsp. pepper

Layer the ingredients in the order given into a wide-mouth 1-quart canning jar. Mix and place the seasonings in a plastic bag. Place the packet on top of the flour.

Attach a gift tag with the cooking instructions.

English Beef Pot Pie

1 jar English Beef Pot Pie Mix
1/4 C. butter or margarine
2 lbs. stew beef
3/4 C. shortening
1 egg
1/2 C. whole milk

In a sauté pan, brown stew beef in butter. Once browned, leave fat in pan and add seasoning packet to form a pasty gravy base. Stir in 4 cups water and bring to a boil; transfer to slow cooker. Cook on high for 1 1/2 hours. In a large mixing bowl, cut shortening into remaining jar ingredients. Whisk egg and milk into mixture then knead a few times with hands (use flour if necessary to keep from sticking). Roll out dough and cut into squares. Arrange dough squares over stew to cover. Cook on high for an additional 1 1/2 hours.

English Beef Pot Pie

1 jar English Beef Pot Pie Mix   3/4 C. shortening
1/4 C. butter or margarine   1 egg
2 lbs. stew beef   1/2 C. whole milk

    In a sauté pan, brown stew beef in butter. Once browned, leave fat in pan and add seasoning packet to form a pasty gravy base. Stir in 4 cups water and bring to a boil; transfer to slow cooker. Cook on high for 1 1/2 hours. In a large mixing bowl, cut shortening into remaining jar ingredients. Whisk egg and milk into mixture then knead a few times with hands (use flour if necessary to keep from sticking). Roll out dough and cut into squares. Arrange dough squares over stew to cover. Cook on high for an additional 1 1/2 hours.

English Beef Pot Pie

1 jar English Beef Pot Pie Mix   3/4 C. shortening
1/4 C. butter or margarine   1 egg
2 lbs. stew beef   1/2 C. whole milk

    In a sauté pan, brown stew beef in butter. Once browned, leave fat in pan and add seasoning packet to form a pasty gravy base. Stir in 4 cups water and bring to a boil; transfer to slow cooker. Cook on high for 1 1/2 hours. In a large mixing bowl, cut shortening into remaining jar ingredients. Whisk egg and milk into mixture then knead a few times with hands (use flour if necessary to keep from sticking). Roll out dough and cut into squares. Arrange dough squares over stew to cover. Cook on high for an additional 1 1/2 hours.

English Beef Pot Pie

1 jar English Beef Pot Pie Mix   3/4 C. shortening
1/4 C. butter or margarine   1 egg
2 lbs. stew beef   1/2 C. whole milk

    In a sauté pan, brown stew beef in butter. Once browned, leave fat in pan and add seasoning packet to form a pasty gravy base. Stir in 4 cups water and bring to a boil; transfer to slow cooker. Cook on high for 1 1/2 hours. In a large mixing bowl, cut shortening into remaining jar ingredients. Whisk egg and milk into mixture then knead a few times with hands (use flour if necessary to keep from sticking). Roll out dough and cut into squares. Arrange dough squares over stew to cover. Cook on high for an additional 1 1/2 hours.

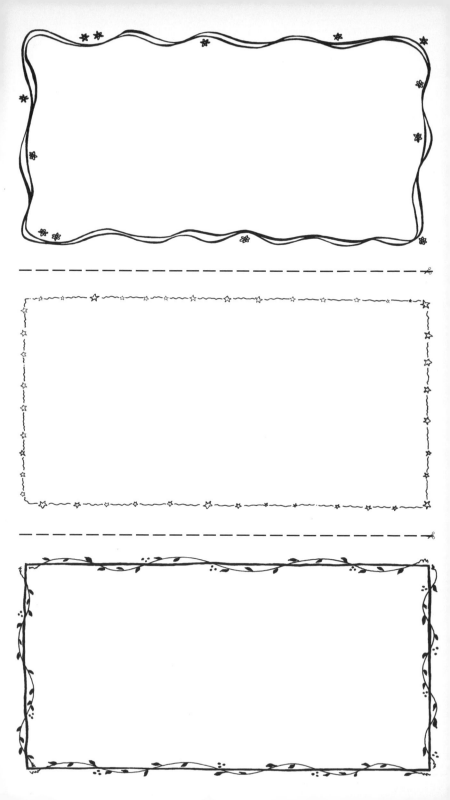

English Beef Pot Pie

1 jar English Beef Pot Pie Mix   3/4 C. shortening
1/4 C. butter or margarine   1 egg
2 lbs. stew beef   1/2 C. whole milk

In a sauté pan, brown stew beef in butter. Once browned, leave fat in pan and add seasoning packet to form a pasty gravy base. Stir in 4 cups water and bring to a boil; transfer to slow cooker. Cook on high for 1 1/2 hours. In a large mixing bowl, cut shortening into remaining jar ingredients. Whisk egg and milk into mixture then knead a few times with hands (use flour if necessary to keep from sticking). Roll out dough and cut into squares. Arrange dough squares over stew to cover. Cook on high for an additional 1 1/2 hours.

English Beef Pot Pie

1 jar English Beef Pot Pie Mix   3/4 C. shortening
1/4 C. butter or margarine   1 egg
2 lbs. stew beef   1/2 C. whole milk

In a sauté pan, brown stew beef in butter. Once browned, leave fat in pan and add seasoning packet to form a pasty gravy base. Stir in 4 cups water and bring to a boil; transfer to slow cooker. Cook on high for 1 1/2 hours. In a large mixing bowl, cut shortening into remaining jar ingredients. Whisk egg and milk into mixture then knead a few times with hands (use flour if necessary to keep from sticking). Roll out dough and cut into squares. Arrange dough squares over stew to cover. Cook on high for an additional 1 1/2 hours.

English Beef Pot Pie

1 jar English Beef Pot Pie Mix   3/4 C. shortening
1/4 C. butter or margarine   1 egg
2 lbs. stew beef   1/2 C. whole milk

In a sauté pan, brown stew beef in butter. Once browned, leave fat in pan and add seasoning packet to form a pasty gravy base. Stir in 4 cups water and bring to a boil; transfer to slow cooker. Cook on high for 1 1/2 hours. In a large mixing bowl, cut shortening into remaining jar ingredients. Whisk egg and milk into mixture then knead a few times with hands (use flour if necessary to keep from sticking). Roll out dough and cut into squares. Arrange dough squares over stew to cover. Cook on high for an additional 1 1/2 hours.

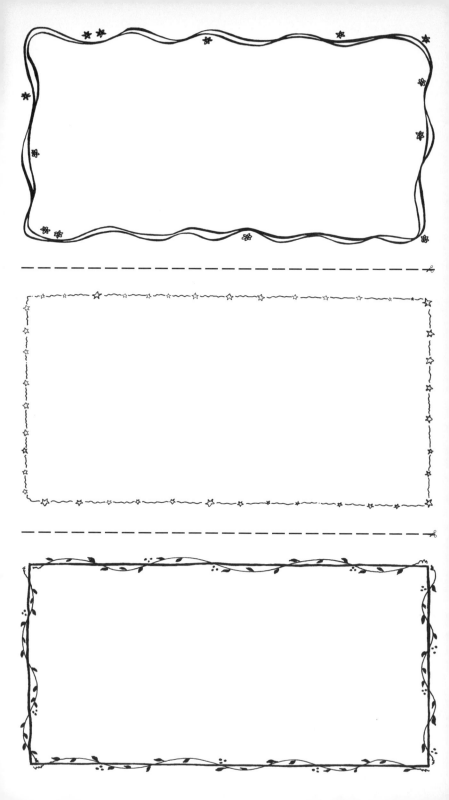

Sage & Apple Stuffing Mix

1/4 C. real bacon bits
1 T. dried minced onion
2 T. dried celery flakes
1 tsp. dried parsley
1/2 tsp. dried thyme
1 bay leaf (place down the side
   of the jar)
1 tsp. dried sage
1 T. chicken bouillon
3 3/4 C. store-bought
   unseasoned bread cubes

Layer the ingredients in the order given into a wide-mouth 1-quart canning jar. Pack each layer into place before adding the next ingredient.

Attach a gift tag with the cooking instructions.

❀ *For a special touch, attach a wooden spoon to the jar.* ❀

Sage & Apple Stuffing

1 jar Sage & Apple Stuffing Mix
2 tart apples, peeled & diced
1/4 C. butter or margarine

Butter bottom and sides of slow cooker. Empty contents of jar into slow cooker, stirring to combine. Add apples to crock and stir. In a saucepan, bring butter and 1 1/4 C. water to a boil. Pour over stuffing mix and stir to combine. Cook on high for 1 1/2 to 2 hours or on low for 3 to 4 hours. Remove and discard bay leaf.

Sage & Apple Stuffing

**1 jar Sage & Apple Stuffing Mix 1/4 C. butter or margarine
2 tart apples, peeled & diced**

Butter bottom and sides of slow cooker. Empty contents of jar into slow cooker, stirring to combine. Add apples to crock and stir. In a saucepan, bring butter and 1 1/4 C. water to a boil. Pour over stuffing mix and stir to combine. Cook on high for 1 1/2 to 2 hours or on low for 3 to 4 hours. Remove and discard bay leaf.

Sage & Apple Stuffing

**1 jar Sage & Apple Stuffing Mix 1/4 C. butter or margarine
2 tart apples, peeled & diced**

Butter bottom and sides of slow cooker. Empty contents of jar into slow cooker, stirring to combine. Add apples to crock and stir. In a saucepan, bring butter and 1 1/4 C. water to a boil. Pour over stuffing mix and stir to combine. Cook on high for 1 1/2 to 2 hours or on low for 3 to 4 hours. Remove and discard bay leaf.

Sage & Apple Stuffing

**1 jar Sage & Apple Stuffing Mix 1/4 C. butter or margarine
2 tart apples, peeled & diced**

Butter bottom and sides of slow cooker. Empty contents of jar into slow cooker, stirring to combine. Add apples to crock and stir. In a saucepan, bring butter and 1 1/4 C. water to a boil. Pour over stuffing mix and stir to combine. Cook on high for 1 1/2 to 2 hours or on low for 3 to 4 hours. Remove and discard bay leaf.

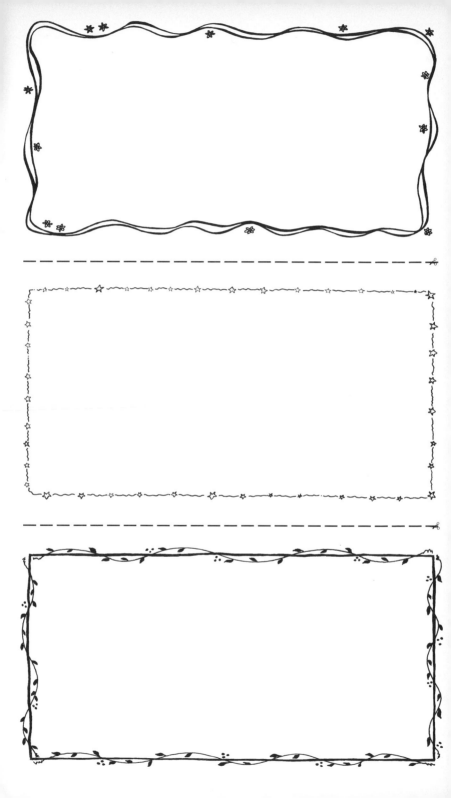

Sage & Apple Stuffing

**1 jar Sage & Apple Stuffing Mix   1/4 C. butter or margarine
2 tart apples, peeled & diced**

Butter bottom and sides of slow cooker. Empty contents of jar into slow cooker, stirring to combine. Add apples to crock and stir. In a saucepan, bring butter and 1 1/4 C. water to a boil. Pour over stuffing mix and stir to combine. Cook on high for 1 1/2 to 2 hours or on low for 3 to 4 hours. Remove and discard bay leaf.

Sage & Apple Stuffing

**1 jar Sage & Apple Stuffing Mix   1/4 C. butter or margarine
2 tart apples, peeled & diced**

Butter bottom and sides of slow cooker. Empty contents of jar into slow cooker, stirring to combine. Add apples to crock and stir. In a saucepan, bring butter and 1 1/4 C. water to a boil. Pour over stuffing mix and stir to combine. Cook on high for 1 1/2 to 2 hours or on low for 3 to 4 hours. Remove and discard bay leaf.

Sage & Apple Stuffing

**1 jar Sage & Apple Stuffing Mix   1/4 C. butter or margarine
2 tart apples, peeled & diced**

Butter bottom and sides of slow cooker. Empty contents of jar into slow cooker, stirring to combine. Add apples to crock and stir. In a saucepan, bring butter and 1 1/4 C. water to a boil. Pour over stuffing mix and stir to combine. Cook on high for 1 1/2 to 2 hours or on low for 3 to 4 hours. Remove and discard bay leaf.

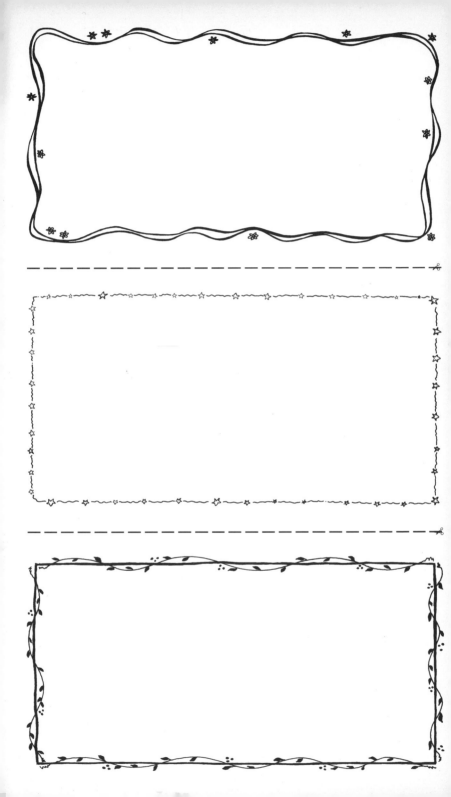